LAUNCH

LARGE-SCALE

LIBRARY INITIATIVES

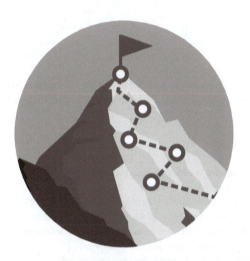

INNOVATION *and* COLLABORATION

VALERIE HORTON

ALA
Editions
CHICAGO | 2021

VALERIE HORTON is a library consultant. She has served as the director of two library consortia: Minitex and the Colorado Library Consortium. She was also the library director at Colorado Mesa University, and worked at New Mexico State University and Brown University. In 2018 she was awarded the ASCLA's Leadership and Professional Achievement Award. Horton received an ALA International Fellowship to automate libraries in the Republic of Trinidad and Tobago. She has coauthored two books for the American Library Association and was the co-general editor of the journal *Collaborative Librarianship*.

© 2021 by Valerie Horton

Extensive effort has gone into ensuring the reliability of the information in this book; however, the publisher makes no warranty, express or implied, with respect to the material contained herein.

ISBN: 978-0-8389-4987-0 (paper)

Library of Congress Cataloging-in-Publication Data
Names: Horton, Valerie, author.
Title: Launching large-scale library initiatives : innovation and collaboration / Valerie Horton.
Description: Chicago : ALA Editions, 2021. | Includes bibliographical references and index. | Summary: "This book provides tips and ideas for libraries to envision, launch, and manage large-scale, innovative projects"—Provided by publisher.
Identifiers: LCCN 2020058693 | ISBN 9780838949870 (paperback)
Subjects: LCSH: Library administration. | Library planning. | Project management.
Classification: LCC Z678 .H68 2021 | DDC 025.1—dc23
LC record available at https://lccn.loc.gov/2020058693

Composition by Alejandra Diaz in the Questa and Bicyclette typefaces.
Cover design by Kimberly Hudgins.

♾ This paper meets the requirements of ANSI/NISO Z39.48-1992 (Permanence of Paper).

Printed in the United States of America
25 24 23 22 21   5 4 3 2 1

LAUNCHING LARGE-SCALE
LIBRARY INITIATIVES

TO MY LIBRARY
FRIENDS AND COLLEAGUES.

*Thank you for sharing the joy,
the hard work, and all those many
learning experiences.*

CONTENTS

ONE

GOING FAR TOGETHER

WELCOME!

Libraries serve communities and communities change.

—SARAH HASHEMI SCOTT ET AL.

"Libraries are not innovative, and librarians are not willing to change." These two myths have been bouncing around our profession for a long time, probably since Melvil Dewey's time. The Stodgy Library Myth is not helpful, and it doesn't take much to disprove it. Just scratch the surface at any public, academic, or school library and you will find makerspaces, coding classes, video production studios, scholarly publishing, kids' yoga, resume workshops, and community gardens. Innovative libraries teach skills and enrich lives while checking out human skeletons, network hubs, cake pans, Santa suits, and geological specimens. Creative activities in libraries happen because library staff are changing along with their communities.

Library science is a proud profession with a record of adapting that would compare favorably to any profession. Over the last decades we have learned a lot about innovation, collaboration, and risk-taking. For example, ALA Editions has published more than thirteen books with the word *innovation* in the title, and twice that many with *collaboration*. A search of the library literature finds more than a thousand academic articles on innovation, while collaboration has nearly two thousand entries. The evidence is clear: librarians are committed to exploring and sharing information about innovation and collaboration. The recent pandemic has forced introspection and change on library staff, but as always, librarians adapt.

What is the place for a book geared toward using innovation and collaboration to manage large-scale library initiatives? Librarians are already innovating within their institutions. What is missing from the literature is a comprehensive examination of how to envision, launch, and manage large-scale, innovative projects across institutions. Working at a large scale adds complexity and specialized knowledge that are not required by librarians who focus on a single institution. If you wish to do something remarkable within our profession, you need to understand what drives transformative and disruptive innovation, and you need to understand how the complexity of large-scale project management requires additional planning, knowledge, and political considerations.

Librarians are innovating within the walls of our institutions, and the skills learned within each institution have great value. There is a growing awareness that to truly keep the profession moving forward in turbulent times, library staff need to work on a bigger playing field. In an age when libraries are once again reinventing themselves, the successful libraries will not be those that turn inward. In explaining his investment strategies, Warren Buffett said that "we simply attempt to be fearful when others are greedy and to be greedy only when others are fearful." Now when most of us are fearful, it is the time to grab the opportunity to change the status quo by reaching for large, progressive visions of the future.

This book borrows heavily on research and theoretical models developed outside the library field. Libraries are often intimate places, and so the direct experience of working at a large scale across multiple institutions is not widely known within the profession. Theories from researchers like Clayton Christensen, Amy Edmondson, and Everett Rogers and business influencers like Steven Johnson, Bill Gates, and Guy Kawasaki are presented in this book, along with information on how to adapt those constructs to the library environment. This book will guide you through the basics of ideation, project management, political pitfalls, preparing for problems, and concepts you probably haven't considered before. When you are finished, you will have the tools you need to meet one of the most difficult challenges within the profession today—planning and launching large-scale library initiatives.

TIPPING THE SCALE

Scalar emphasis has become an important question for libraries.

—LORCAN DEMPSEY

What does it mean to work at scale? In general, *at scale* is another term for *scalability*, or the ability to apply additional resources or capacity to a system to handle expanding workload. A well-scaled system is flexible enough to maintain efficient performance as demands on resources increase.

In computer science, *scalability* means to create systems that are capable of massive or rapid growth to encompass increasing demand. Think about the growth required by companies like Zoom which had to manage an avalanche of online meeting requests during the recent pandemic. In an economic context, a scalable business model has the ability to add more resources, such as the ability to add more trucks during an increase in shipping loads. The determination as to whether a new library project or service can be expanded or upgraded to accommodate greater patron demand is an important part of designing new library initiatives. In principle, scalability goes up and down the library spectrum, with some ideas being handled best at the institution level and others through a regional or national approach.

A related concept is "economies of scale." The concept of economies of scale is used by economists in situations where the average cost of doing business decreases as the output increases. Those who run library couriers know that as more books ship between libraries, the cost of moving a single book decreases. Economy of scale is one of the most important benefits of doing larger projects. In libraries, the classic example of economy of scale is those libraries lucky enough to have negotiated statewide database packages. In the aggregate, those libraries pay much less for the same products than states where each library negotiates its own vendor contracts. For example, Minnesota libraries pay less per database use because their statewide contract includes North and South Dakota's libraries. Vendors will lower the price per person as headcounts increase, so larger negotiating pools save libraries money.

Working at a large scale provides fertile ground for innovation to develop. Innovation proponents like Steven Johnson and Bill Gates argue that innovation occurs when unexpected connections are made, and surprising ideas can collide together. This innovation crucible is built when people working toward a common goal bring different approaches to the table in the early ideation stage. Insular libraries do not reap the benefit of connecting staff from different organizations and unique perspectives together.

Another potential advantage of working at scale is resilience, the ability to recover quickly from difficulties. Resilience is becoming an increasingly important concept in the social sciences and business fields. For a system to be able to work across multiple libraries and geographic distances, it needs an established knowledge base, solid leadership, robust procedures, and strong interpersonal relationships. To build a stable foundation for a new project, the participants will have had to develop the tools and agreements necessary to make the collaboration work, and that helps create a resilient system.

Members of library consortia will tell you that one of the major advantages of working collaboratively is getting to know library staff outside their home institutions. The relationships built in cooperative projects improve the skills and knowledge of local staff members, expand opportunities for creative ideas to occur, and demonstrate to funders that the library is a good steward of public funds. There are also opportunities to earn solid publicity from joint projects. For example, look at the spectacular publicity the Digital Public Library of America (DPLA) earned during its 2013 launch.

There are also intangible benefits in large-scale collaboration, as illustrated by HathiTrust, a nonprofit group of academic and research libraries which has preserved more than 17 million digitized books and other items. HathiTrust asserts that serving the public good is its mission. Its web page says that the organization is committed to contributing "to research, scholarship, and the common good by collaboratively collecting, organizing, preserving, communicating, and sharing the record of human knowledge." Preserving the record of human knowledge is no small undertaking. HathiTrust goes a long way to proving that working on large-scale projects can profoundly change the world in ways that librarians back in Melvil Dewey's time couldn't have dreamed of.

COMPLEXITY, WE GOT THAT

I think the next century will be the century of complexity.

—STEPHEN HAWKING

There are many advantages to working on the large end of the spectrum, but there are also times when working on large-scale initiatives can multiply problems as well. Big, new projects are going to be complex, and the larger the scale the more complex they will be. Strong leadership is required and is not always available. Library project managers will need to create robust procedures, infrastructure, and resource bases to handle the issues that come up when working with geographically separated institutions that have different norms, operating styles, and achievement needs. The reverse is also true: sometimes projects are scaled too small to be effective. In the example used earlier, given North Dakota's total population of 750,000, the entire state would be unlikely to negotiate as good a price as the Austin Public Library in Texas can achieve on its own.

Working at scale generally requires a large resource base. Those resources include money, facilities, materials, people, time, commitment, and energy. No library has these resources in abundance. Working at scale can allow a more manageable commitment of resources across many libraries. However, large projects can also have budgets that seem to grow with abandon. We have seen many library organizations like the Digital Preservation Network or OCLC's former regional systems close or merge due to a strained resource base. If your library project is aimed at a large regional audience, you will need to know the competing consortia in your area and see if collaboration with your project is possible.

One of the biggest dangers in project management is "scope creep." This is the seemingly inevitable force that pushes any project beyond its original design or goals. Cornelius Fichtner said that "there is no such thing as scope creep, only scope gallop." Any experienced project manager would readily agree with Fichtner. In my experience, library projects produce an endless number of requests for add-ons and changes that bump up costs and bring delays.

Library leadership changes can be another problem area. During an interview for the post of director of the largest academic library in a regional consortium, the question I was asked most often was whether I would keep the library in that local consortium. The interviewers' fear about this was palpable. A major leadership change among the institutions in your cooperative endeavor can be one of the most dangerous moments in a project's life cycle, and one you probably won't have much ability to affect.

Like most things, working at scale has both pros and cons. In general, I haven't included obstacles that you can't control, in order not to worry you. But these obstacles can sometimes have just the opposite effect. It can be liberating to know that there is only so much you can do, and all you need to do is to *stay calm and push on* despite the obstacles you will encounter.

If you want to do something amazing, try to think like Bill Gates, who often tells people not to let complexity stop forward momentum. If your goal is to improve your library's functionality and how it is perceived by your patrons and funders, then working on an innovative, large-scale, collaborative project will get you the best bang for your buck. Regarding his grand challenge to eliminate global poverty and disease, Bill Gates said, "[this is] why I am so passionate about the broader process of innovation. Because we do not always succeed. But when we do, we can exceed even our best-case scenarios." That is a good reason for any librarian to embrace both innovation and collaboration.

RIGHT-SIZED PROJECTS

Libraries face interesting choices about sourcing—local, commercial, collaborative, public—as they look at how to achieve goals, and as shared approaches become more crucial as resources are stretched.

—LORCAN DEMPSEY

Lorcan Dempsey has pondered "scalar emphasis," or the level at which it make sense to get things done. He sees library initiatives as fitting into one of four levels of scalar emphasis:

- Institutional (individual library)
- Group (regional, consortium)
- Public entity (state, country)
- Web scale (national, international, or commercial network services provided by companies like Amazon and Google)

Dempsey identified a clear trend toward externalization, in which more activities are being done collaboratively or are being outsourced entirely. He also argues that many projects might include several different levels of scalar emphasis. For instance, training may be done in the institution, software development at the consortium level, and network maintenance outsourced to the Web.

"Right scaling," according to Dempsey, means choosing the appropriate source for the work that is needed to be done. For patron-focused tasks, the institutional scale is still appropriate, especially in areas of patron services and outreach. Other services, however, are more efficiently done at the regional or consortial level. George Needham believes that there is no longer any excuse for libraries duplicating work *on* anything. Needham argues that anything that can be done by a collective, should be done collectively.

Dempsey points out that we already do many things at "web scale." We buy our databases, get our network server farms, and access software through the internet. We reap all the advantages of sharing resources across massive user pools. Across the country, resource-sharing pools take advantage of scale at large consortia like Minitex, OhioLINK, and the Massachusetts Library System. There are also a growing number of vendor systems that are designed to share work at the national or international level. OCLC's WorldShare Management System and ExLibris's Alma use one segmented catalog for all library collections held across thousands of libraries. HathiTrust and the DPLA are examples of national efforts to share massive amounts of digital content from hundreds or thousands of institutions.

Scalar emphasis is often not specifically identified in many project plans, but it should be, along with cost, staffing resources, impact, facilities, and so on. The right scale for doing the work should be a standard analysis component of any project. By acknowledging that scale is as critical as cost or staff requirements, library managers can add dimension to their planning and potentially expand the options available in their decision-making. This book will focus on regional, mega-regional, and national-scale projects. Large-scale initiatives are always collaborative projects.

GOING FURTHER TOGETHER

Bad libraries build collections, good libraries build services, great libraries build communities.

—R. DAVID LANKES

At the most fundamental level, I believe that libraries are creative, change-oriented organizations. For some library professionals, there are plenty of opportunities to meet others, go to conferences, give presentations, sit on committees, or simply share coffee with colleagues from neighboring institutions. These opportunities may not be available to some of their colleagues, however. Most library professionals know they must get out into their communities, whether that is a classroom, a faculty meeting, the local service club, or a city council meeting. Libraries are strongest when they push into the community and focus outward rather than only serving those who walk in the door.

In my experience, most people think that the primary value of working collaboratively is saving money. Using resources wisely is a great value, of course, but a 2012 OCLC study of more than 100 library consortium leaders found that the main advantage in belonging to a collaborative was professional networking (30 percent), followed by cost savings (23 percent), access to e-content (12 percent), shared catalogs (12 percent), and resource-sharing (11 percent). If a library staff member is working outside the walls of their institution, that person is being exposed to new ideas, new challenges, and new ways of thinking. The best library employee is the one who has the broadest worldview, and the best way to get that wider worldview is to build structures, like large-scale projects, that enable staff to interact across many diverse organizations.

Research by Stephen Johnson and others has revealed that innovation and creativity are attributes that grow and thrive in stimulating environments. Great ideas are born when different people, ideas, norms, and challenges mix and generate collisions of ideas and concepts. The most creative project I managed involved librarians pushing beyond their natural boundaries. We launched the Minnesota Libraries Publishing Project in 2018, a joint venture of academic libraries, library consortia, and public libraries. We made a high-quality book self-publishing tool available to every resident in Minnesota through their local library. The Minitex consortium managed the infrastructure, the academic libraries paid for the publishing platform, and the public libraries paid for Indie Minnesota, a digital collection of local authors whereby any self-published book could be made available statewide. The public libraries also sponsored self-published book contests. School librarians published their schools' manuals, and cultural heritage organizations supported the publishing of local histories. We can do so much more together.

This project is a perfect example of how innovation, scale, and serendipity can come together to produce amazing results. In times like these, when the value of the library itself is being called into question, we need to show our impact. Innovation and collaboration are tools that help libraries improve services, redesign products, and offer opportunities that can impact, and indeed transform, people's lives and their concept of a library. In a time of crisis like the pandemic, the instinctive reaction is to pull back and focus on the home institution. That is exactly the wrong approach. Now is the perfect time to shake up the status quo and push out. We need to hold fast to the adage: "To go fast, go alone. To go far, go together."

EMBRACING PROJECT MANAGEMENT

Trying to manage a project without project management is like trying to play a football game without a game plan.

—KATHERINE TATE

If you are doing a small project, you probably will not need to use project management tools or processes. A spreadsheet and a word processor will get the job done. But if you are working on a large-scale project, you will have no choice but to adopt project management techniques. The *Encyclopedia of Management* defines "project management" as applying reasoning and tools for planning, controlling, and managing a short-term endeavor.

The experts who study project management have organized its functions into five categories: initiation, planning, execution, monitoring and assessment, and closure. The remaining chapters of this book are organized around those five functions. Librarians new to project management often make the mistake of confusing project management software with project management itself. We'll look at software tools later in the book. For now, you need a grounding in the key concepts of successful project management.

The Initiation or Pre-Planning Stage

Time spent in initiating will pay dividends through the rest of the project.

—CARLY WIGGINS SEARCY

For many, the initiation stage is the fun part of project management. You get to let your imagination run free during the ideation stage while engaging with others and building enthusiasm. All of this can be a joyous ride. This stage is crucial to building the foundations for your grassroots effort, and your goal will be to reach out and connect with as many potential stakeholders and supporters as possible. In the initiation stage you develop your project's scope, justify the need for it, gain tentative approval, and start defining work parameters.

This stage is often referred to as the pre-planning stage, and this is where you begin to identify your goals, build your case, and lay the foundations for later requests for resource allocation. A critical piece of work in the initiation stage is defining the scope of your project, or the parameters of the final product or service you will produce. Controlling scope allows you to manage the project with fewer disruptions and keep the project on a clear trajectory. In this stage, stakeholders make commitments, participants are found, and work responsibilities are starting to be defined. The preliminary analysis you do at this stage on the project's scope, objectives, costs, benefits, time frame, and risks will be fleshed out later during the full planning stage.

One of the common mistakes people make is to not spend enough time on the pre-planning stage. There are a lot of conversations that must happen and concepts that must be explored before committing to launching a large-scale initiative. People also tend to want to get into the details of the project too quickly, without spending time looking at the situation from a 30,000-foot level. The project management expert James P. Lewis argues that the cause of most project failures is laid down during these early definitional stages. You must reach agreement on what your problem is, what you hope to accomplish, and your main strategy to achieve your goals. If you don't have an agreement on those three things, you will meet with endless problems going forward from people working under different assumptions. There is time later to get to the details.

The Planning Stage

One of the major causes of project failures is poor planning.

—JAMES P. LEWIS

In the planning stage, a detailed project plan and a project schedule are created. In this stage details are clarified, research is conducted, costs are identified, and work responsibilities are assigned. In fact, there are myriads of details to address, as outlined later in this book. There are significant issues of maintenance and control that will need to be worked out with many different participants who have various points of view. Communication, always important, becomes critical at this stage. The project manager is constantly struggling to balance on the fine line between releasing too much information and thereby raising unrealistic expectations, and not releasing enough information and thus having the proposal viewed as an information black hole. This is a tough balancing act, but it is a critical one to the project's future success.

Your stakeholders are going to be clamoring to see your work plans, timelines, and budgets. Librarians want details! As the project moves forward, the project schedule you are creating becomes the guidepost that drives the work of the project manager. There are a significant number of tools to help the process like Gantt charts, PERT, CPM, and so on.

Several dangers can occur at this stage. The planning can bog down and drain away enthusiasm. A weak planning document or inadequate communication can drive away stakeholders and potential participants. The new working groups or teams must find a way to become cohesive and productive. As mentioned earlier, inexperienced project managers often try to get by with minimal planning. Excited participants want to jump into the work before the plan is complete, and this can mean that the preparation stage is so poorly executed that your project can start to veer off track as it matures. During the planning stage, the key is to keep things moving while ensuring that the quality of the work remains high and that communication does not falter.

The Execution Stage

Plans are only good intentions unless they immediately degenerate into hard work.

—PETER DRUCKER

Execution is the stage where the work gets done; resources are gathered and expended; contracts are signed; products or services are developed and tested; and web pages, training, and public relations materials are created. All these steps in the plan are now taking place, and necessary adjustments are being made. This stage is all about managing people and resources while coordinating the plan activities across different working groups and communicating, always communicating. The execution stage often involves internal testing, a pilot project, and a public launch. The project manager needs to make sure that all the teams and subcontractors are performing, and that resources are available to continue the work plan.

This is also the stage where scope creep happens, where changes to the initial project design start adding cost overruns and schedule delays. Things are happening fast and decisions are being made while the critical documentation of decisions gets forgotten, causing problems later. In hindsight, most project managers will say the execution stage is never quite what they anticipated. It can either move shockingly fast or bog down due to unanticipated problems. Reporting out gains more importance as the work progresses.

The execution stage is when the project manager is controlling the multiple functions being carried out by different entities. The project manager, along with a steering committee, has major responsibility for controlling the project's scope, schedule, and budget.

The Monitoring and Assessment Stage

No major project is ever installed on time, within budget, with the same staff that started it.

—JOHN RUSSELL ET AL.

The project is launched, course corrections are being made, and the product is being integrated into existing services. Now you are switching over to monitoring and controlling the project as it moves into stabilization. This is the stage where you assess how different your finished product is from what your plan said it would be, and ask if anything needs to be done to get the project closer to the intended outcome. There are other questions you will need to ask, including:

- Was the work done of high quality and acceptable quantity as compared to your original concept?

- Did you meet your budget, timelines, goals, and objectives?
- Did you stay within your project scope?
- Have you documented all the work that was done and the decisions made?
- Are there significant changes still to be made?

There are lessons to be learned at this stage that will be invaluable to you in future project management activities. The assessment activities at this stage are focused on the process used to create the project; you will assess how well you met your outcome goals in the next stage.

Project management gurus call this phase "monitoring and control," though the literature has a fair amount of variation in defining the exact terminology. As Carly Wiggins Searcy points out, in some ways monitoring and control are occurring throughout the project and so may not need a special phase. But given that library projects use public funding and must justify that the funds are well spent, I believe that monitoring and assessment require special consideration. The assessment of the work done is likely to require significant space in all reports that are created and shared with stakeholders and other auditing organizations.

The Closure Stage

A project is complete when it starts working for you, rather than you are working for it.

—SCOTT ALLEN

At some point the project is over, and the new service or product is being used by library staff and patrons. Carly Wiggins Searcy has said that this is the part of the project everyone ignores if they can get away with it. I have been guilty of that, but you should recall that part of the definition of project management is that it comes to an end, and there are closeout activities that need to be done. Three remaining tasks are:

1. Assess how the outcome worked for the intended users.
2. Create a final project document.
3. Turn the work over to the staff who will continue to maintain and support the product.

If possible, your closeout activities should be undertaken by the same project staff and the steering committee who oversaw the initiative. Unfortunately, large-scale projects usually take time, and many people will have moved on since your work started.

There are many questions to ask at this stage: What do users, staff, and stakeholders think of the product? What "lessons learned" can you carry forward to the next project? By far the most important questions, however, have to do with outcomes. Has something significant changed for those who interact with your product or service? Assessment outcomes are difficult to analyze and are explored in the last chapter of this book.

The managed turnover of the work includes documenting the vast number of decisions that were made before you turn the project over to the group that will maintain it over time. Make sure to thank those who gave sweat-equity to the project. Celebration works well for those who value tradition and appreciate a successful handover ritual. Many people don't like the pomp, but it serves as a clear demarcation of the status change. You will be transitioning activities to a group that will be assigned to continue to oversee the results of your project. You know you have closure when you add the project to your resume!

THE END OF THE BEGINNING

The proverb "To go fast, go alone. To go far, go together," has been a crucial part of my professional philosophy for years. It distills a great lesson in a few words. Most of the time in a librarian's career, you must move fast and get things done. Fine, do that!

But this book is about those other times, those memorable times when you want to make a significant impact on our profession. The times when going big allows you to do something remarkable and noteworthy. Once you make that decision, it immediately follows that you will need to use a collaborative framework to get needed resources. It also means you're going to need to use the techniques and tools associated with project management. This rest of this book will guide you through the stages of refining your idea, planning, executing, monitoring, and assessing the outcome.

When I look back at my career, I greatly value the day-to-day work of managing libraries and consortia. However, what I treasure most were the large-scale projects where I worked with others to push what was perceived as normal within the profession. To give you an idea of where the experiences came from that I've drawn upon for this book, here is a list of the large-scale projects I have either directed or collaborated on. I have:

- Loaded periodical MARC records directly into an online catalog in 1992, a decade before it was a norm
- Launched an open-source online catalog for over sixty libraries in Colorado (2005)
- Cleaned up the most popular Project Gutenberg MARC records that were downloaded by more than 3,000 libraries worldwide (2013)
- Created the earliest statewide e-book platforms running on the then 3M e-book platform in Colorado (2009)
- Worked with the DPLA as one of its six founding digital collections (2013)
- Worked on the development and launched SimplyE in Minnesota (2016)
- Developed a statewide self-publishing platform in Minnesota (2018)

These are the experiences that remain with me as the years have gone by. This book was written to help others take that leap into working at scale on innovative initiatives within our profession.

REFERENCES

Allan, Barbara. *The No-Nonsense Guide to Project Management*. London: Facet, 2017.

Daugherty, Alice, and Samantha Hines. *Project Management in the Library Workplace*. Bingley, UK: Emerald, 2018.

Dempsey, Lorcan, and Kenneth J. Varnum. *The Network Reshapes the Library: Lorcan Dempsey on Libraries, Services, and Networks*. London: Facet, 2014.

Harper, Val. "Rightsizing Project Management for Libraries." *Library Leadership & Management* 32 (January 2018): 1–11.

Lewis, James P. *Fundamentals of Project Management*. 4th ed. New York: American Management Association, 2007.

Needham, George. "Bottling the Collaboration Thing." *Collaborative Librarianship* 7 (2015): 2.

OCLC. "U.S. Library Consortia: A Snapshot of Priorities & Perspectives." 2012.

Searcy, Carly Wiggins. *Project Management in Libraries: On Time, On Budget, On Target*. Chicago: American Library Association, 2018.

TWO

SCOPE, SCALE, AND OTHER SURVIVAL GUIDES

SCOPE: IT'S A THING

Identifying what is outside the scope of the project helps to develop a tight project boundary.

—BARBARA ALLEN

When working on large-scale initiatives, scope is a big deal. Scope is not one of the topics you hear mentioned all that often in library circles, much like scale as discussed in the previous chapter. However, even in the earliest ideation or pre-planning stage, scope is crucial to reaching shared understandings. In this context, scope sets the parameters and defines the actions you are going to take to reach the completion of the project.

In the main, a scope statement is an agreement between the stakeholders and the project staff on what will be accomplished. It serves the critical role of making sure that everyone is on the same page and moving in the same direction. The terms of your scope statement must be agreed upon before starting work on the project. While not a typical practice in libraries, in the business world stakeholders and project staff often sign the scope statement to show they have reached an agreement. Signing a scope statement says that the problem you are working on is important enough to justify the actions to be taken.

Scope management includes authorizing the job, defining the boundaries of the project, subdividing the work into manageable components, identifying success outcomes, and specifying change control parameters. The scope statement needs to answer the following questions:

- What problem will be solved by the project?
- Why is doing this project of specific benefit to library patrons or staff?
- Does this idea push forward the future of libraries?
- Who are the project's logical stakeholders, users, trainers, influencers, and promoters?
- Are there time limits or constraints on the project?

Questions like these will need to be hashed out with your pre-planning team, or those people you trust to help you work through early project considerations. Other basic items that need to be included in your scope statement include the project's name, its main objectives and deliverables, the project owner and main stakeholders, the final decision-makers, and the project's exclusions, constraints, and working assumptions.

You should expect to see significant changes in your thinking and goals as you work through the project's scope with stakeholders. This is a time when the opinions of trusted colleagues can be indispensable in helping you see a better path forward. James P. Lewis argues that if you are seeing a lot of change requests as your project progresses, this probably means that you didn't spend enough time up-front defining terms, doing planning, and reaching an agreement. Scope change later in the project is expensive and can destroy budgets and deadlines, and it usually happens because something important was not thought through early in the process. We'll talk about scope creep more in a later chapter, but within any project, there are always pressures to make it bigger, more complex, and more costly. The scope statement can help you keep those pressures to a minimum.

LAYING THE GROUNDWORK

Creativity, the ability to generate novel and useful ideas, is the seed of innovation, but unless it's applied and scaled it's still just an idea.

—DAVID BURKUS

Before we launch into creating your concept and starting your project, we need to look more at scale and laying the groundwork for your project. Bill Gates argues that when working on large-scale projects, you need to think differently compared to developing in-house projects. Gates has reinvented himself as a philanthropist by using data and science to understand large social trends in education, poverty, and health care. He started his philanthropic work in 1995 when his foundation gave 25,000 PCs to 5,800 public libraries while training over 7,000 librarians.

Gates has always been interested in big ideas. He persuasively argues that great ideas do not appear in isolation, which is not an uncommon message. Where he offers a unique insight is by identifying that the main problem is not generating big ideas; the problem is operationalizing those ideas and creating a platform where the ideas can be productive.

Once you have your big idea, the next step is putting that idea into action. According to Gates, when working in the public arena, the act of delivering consistent and high-quality results is difficult and fraught with failure. He argues that to successfully implement a big project, you need to have three essential concepts implemented from the start of your project design. You need to:

1. Choose a scale that is big enough to be truly impactful.
2. Focus intensely on the local situation.
3. Develop a system to measure the results of your work.

Gates's philanthropic work has largely focused on public health, but there is much that libraries can learn from examining his three points.

Make a Big Jump

I'll believe it when I see it. But if you believe it, you can see it. That's how innovation happens. You need to buy in and believe that it works first.

—GUY KAWASAKI

Guy Kawasaki was one of the original designers of the Macintosh personal computers. He argues that the mistake most businesses make is thinking that if they improve their product by 10 percent and drop the price by 10 percent, they will find success. Think of Henry Ford's famous statement that if he had asked people what they wanted, he'd have built a faster horse. Kawasaki agrees and argues that we'd all be using fancier flip phones if incrementalism were the best model for success.

Kawasaki claims that we too often limit ourselves to "I'll believe it when I see it" thinking. That kind of concrete reasoning only allows for incremental improvements and doesn't promote transformational innovation. Innovation is unleashed when you *jump*, not step, into a new vision of the future. If you believe you can achieve something remarkable, you will marshal the energy, the drive, and the resources to do astonishing things. The other key argument Kawasaki makes is to stop paying attention to *how* you do something and focus instead on *what* it is you want to achieve. For libraries, this has proven true throughout our history. If we had decided we were only about print books, we would no longer exist. Libraries are about leisure reading, education support, learning, information, making things, building communities, and transforming lives.

Kawasaki recommends that you keep the project's mission and goals in the forefront of your design discussions. Big projects take a lot of energy, a lot of time, and a lot of commitment. One of your organizing principles needs to be making it worth the time and effort of your stakeholders to participate. Think about the hundreds of libraries that signed up for the HathiTrust Digital Library. They put their resources on the line because they wanted to digitize their academic collections, and the only way to do that was to go big, go innovative, and go collaborative.

This is the beauty—*the genius*—of the big project. You are selling the next jump into the future and that is the best way to generate energy, interest, and resources.

Go Hyper-Local

Great libraries always have great librarians who engage the community and seek to identify and help fulfill the aspirations of that community.

—R. DAVID LANKES

There are many things I admire about libraries. I would place our values against any organization in the world and argue that we are among the best of the best. But of all our many virtues, one stands out for me. Libraries are all about their local communities. Whether that community is a college campus, a rural town, or a suburban high school, libraries develop due to influences that are deeply embedded in their local environment, and they are designed to meet the unique needs of that situation.

Bill Gates's second point for achieving large-scale project success is that projects should not follow cookie-cutter models that worked somewhere else. Your project must be grounded in the local realities of your participating libraries. I made this mistake when I took a successful graduating senior fund-raising campaign from an urban community and tried to apply it in my rural, first-generation college. It was a spectacular failure because it wasn't grounded in the fund-raising norms of my community.

If your project is flexible, you may be surprised by the unforeseen way your system is used by local library staff and patrons. In designing your project, make sure you keep it flexible enough so that participating libraries can customize it to fit their local community's needs. No cookie-cutter solutions! By fostering the ability of each group in your coalition to succeed, you can share what makes sense to do at scale while allowing creativity to flourish within each library. The movie quote that "if you build it, they will come" is true if you leave space for unexpected uses of your work, and honor and support those who use your work as they branch out to meet the needs of their local community.

Measure Early, Measure Often

I have been struck by how important measurement is to improving the human condition. You can achieve incredible progress if you set a clear goal and find a measure that will drive progress toward that goal.

—BILL GATES

Bill Gates speaks about accountability and assessment more often than any other influencer in America. When dissecting his global projects, Gates often refers to how basic assessment is. Yet he is surprised by how seldom assessment is done, and when it is done, how difficult it is to get it right. His basic philosophy is that we all need feedback, because without feedback there can be no improvement.

Academic libraries have been diligently trying to measure outcomes for decades. They recognized the need for budget accountability for higher education administrators and stakeholders. Academic librarians have chosen outcome measures that demonstrate their libraries' contributions to the institution's goals, overall value, and return on the investment. Library services that have been heavily assessed include information literacy's impact on improving student research skills, evaluating the quality and effectiveness of open educational resources, the archival role of the library in the academy, the effectiveness of discovery tools, and the shift from collections to services, to name just a few. Typical assessment activities include pre- and post-testing, surveys, interviews, and the evaluation of student research. Most large academic libraries use one of several available national survey tools, such as Libqual+, Ithaka S+R's US Faculty Survey, the ACRL's Metrics, and the ARL's MINES.

As with academic libraries, public libraries must demonstrate their effectiveness to local government entities. Public libraries have also often struggled to find effective outcome measures. A case in point is from 2018. I led a *Library Journal*–sponsored discussion with public library directors from eight large systems on how they were engaging their creative arts community (musicians, writers, painters, etc.). All of them had high-quality programs to display public art in their buildings. Many held workshops and children's programming to create visual arts. Several had adopted Rabble's MUSICat and were offering works from local musicians online. Many supported NANOWRIMO or had created writers' groups in their branches. Most did a good job of giving these outreach programs lots of media and public attention. It was impressive. But when asked what measures they were taking to judge the effectiveness of their innovative outreach programs, there was no answer beyond attendee head counts, which is an output, not an outcome measure.

This is not to say that public libraries aren't trying to get a handle on outcome assessment. A state librarian told me that public libraries contribute endless data every year to statistical aggregators such as the National Center for Education Statistics' IPEDS and to numerous one-off annual surveys at the behest of state libraries, university researchers, and professional associations. However, she went on to say, there are no effective national composites that describe library use, contribute to learning outcomes, or evaluate the purpose or impact of public libraries on their communities. The effectiveness of aggregated public libraries' outcome measures is only as meaningful as any given library's data collection system, which is often a true hit-or-miss operation. Attempts are now being made to get a broader-based outcome measures system established, including the Public

Library Association's impressive Project Outcome. Other outcomes efforts are being undertaken by state librarians through the Measures that Matter project and by the Research Institute for Public Libraries.

Chapter 11 of this book goes into assessment in detail, but the topic is also included in this chapter for a specific reason. You need to think about how you will evaluate the effectiveness of your project as you design it. The norm in our profession is to build our evaluation structures long after our new product or service has rolled out. This doesn't work in an era where public funding is scarce, and libraries often must make sacrifices to join in large projects. Moreover, as Gates argues, well-designed assessment plans can be part of the selling features of your project. Demonstrating that you are committed to showing the value of your project to potential funders and participants is a power play that we underutilize as a profession.

RIDING OUT THE HARD TIMES

It's fine to celebrate success, but it is more important to heed the lessons of failure.

—BILL GATES

If you are reading this book, you have the moxie to consider doing something remarkable, and large-scale library initiatives are always worthy of being remarked upon. You're going to need skills, fortitude, and resilience to make it through the fun and often frustrating days ahead. This section is designed to give you a chance to think about your skills, your drive, your problem-solving abilities, and your stick-to-it-ness.

Jeff Dyer and his colleagues, who wrote *The Innovator's DNA*, have studied the triggers for people who come up with and implement big ideas. He and his colleagues found that five skills distinguished the most creative business leaders. As you go through the project management stages involved in creating a large-scale project, you should be practicing and fine-tuning these personal skills. The five learnable skills are:

1. *Associating*: The ability to connect two ideas to solve a problem. The more diverse our life experiences and learning opportunities, the more connections we can make. New concepts and ideas trigger divergent thinking, and that can lead to the generation of new ideas.

2. *Questioning*: Given a roadblock, ask yourself: why can't I . . . ? The best project leaders constantly ask provocative and evocative questions. Dyer's research found that innovators deliberately ask questions that stimulate new thinking. The authors recommend asking Why, Why Not, and What If? Don't just accept the first response, and push through especially if you're hearing "we've always done it this way" feedback.

3. *Observing*: What's going on around you? What will work in this environment at this time? Observe your potential users, vendors, and customer service employees. What works? What doesn't? Here is your chance to play detective. Sometimes small behavioral details allow you to gain insights into new ways of doing the work. Direct observation is one of the keys to the famous Toyota Way business development model.

4. *Networking*: Along with observing, networking can give you a platform for gaining different perspectives, along with the ability to test out hypotheses before putting them into action. Try to meet with people who are not in the same library niche that you are. If you're an academic library, visit an innovative public library. If you're a public librarian, go to a cultural heritage library, and so on. There are times when the best solutions can come from outside our profession, so go visit other nonprofit, government, or commercial ventures that inspire you. One of the most successful tools I used during my career was inviting people out to lunch or coffee.

5. *Experimenting*: What small, simple steps can you take to test your ideas? Dyer and his colleagues found that the most innovative business leaders all did some form of active experimentation. Experimentation can be expensive and time-consuming, so use it where you can in quick and simple ways.

The innovators in Dyer's research were big risk-takers. They wanted to make history, change the world, and shake up the status quo. It takes courage to be an innovator and use these five tools. The good news is that the more you use your creative abilities, the better you will get at it. Innovation is not always an innate ability; it is often a learned skill. Dyer argues that if you're looking for a place to begin this journey, start with questions, especially the Why and Why Not ones. Think of these five skills as your secret sauce to make your innovative project stand out from its peers.

Resilience

There is a higher probability that things will accidentally go wrong in a project than that they will accidentally go right.

—JAMES P. LEWIS

Resilience is one of those words that has gained traction in the business and social science literature. Pioneer research done by Norman Garmezy was summarized in a book by Paul Tough in 2012 called *How Children Succeed.* The researchers found that children who survived and thrived despite difficult circumstances were not the smartest, but those who did not give up. The children who developed a wide range of coping skills and remained stubbornly focused on their personal goals were the ones who succeeded in life despite facing terrible obstacles.

Formal definitions of *resilience* tend to include concepts like the ability to recover quickly from misfortune or the elastic ability to return to an original shape. Slang definitions can be more apt, and a word like *grit* is used to mean firmness, pluck, or strong character. All of these traits are admirable, but from the library project management perspective, the most important trait is resilience. Resilience is the ability to survive, adapt, and thrive in the face of adversity. Resilience is often tied to businesses, economies, or communities facing some natural or man-made catastrophe. The literature is filled with articles on how to build flexible, healthy, and sustainable organizations and systems.

Job descriptions for project managers often list resilience as one of the key traits they are looking for in new hires. Experienced project managers have learned that things can go wrong in every large-scale project, so what is important is how you deal with that fact. If you leave this book with only one takeaway, I hope it will be the knowledge that project management is tough, and any veteran of the experience will understand that and be inclined to support you. It's the newbies and the bright-eyed enthusiasts who naively assume that project management is easy.

Many writers focus on resilience as if it were a muscle that can be strengthened by use, and they are correct. Knowing the techniques of resilience will be an asset in your management skills toolkit. There are numerous resilience and grit training programs offered by companies like LinkedIn Learning, Coursera, and the NROC Project. TED Talks are overflowing with clever talks about building resilience, and you can find multitudes of books on the topic, including my two favorites, *Rising Strong* by Brené Brown and *Learned Optimism* by Martin Seligman. You should also look at information connected to emotional intelligence, which shares many similar concepts and techniques.

For now, you should know that resilience is *not* the tenacity to tough it out. The ability to tough things out is grit and is a valuable trait to have. Resilience training focuses more on learning not to blame yourself to the point of incapacitation when things go wrong. Instead, look for ways to bounce back in the face of adversity. Your goal should be to mimic that famous World War II poster, "Keep calm and carry on." You may not be feeling calm in a crisis, but you can act as if you are.

Another trait identified with resilience is the ability to act and react quickly. When things go wrong, don't freeze. Pull out the contingency plan, get on the phone and ask for advice, reassure your teams, and above all—do something! Whether you believe that things will be fine is irrelevant; any experienced manager will tell you there are times when you need to project confidence and belief in your project's success. Others will appreciate your efforts even if they are skeptical of your ability to pull a rabbit out of the project budget. I am not recommending that you jump without consideration, but don't put off action. It can help to center yourself back into the project's mission and values. If you speak from principle, people will listen and wish to help you move forward.

You are going to face many demands, and you will work with others who don't perform as promised. It can be aggravating to work with people who don't understand the process but feel as if they can judge you. Those demonstrating resilience strive to retain a positive attitude, empathy for the inexperienced, emotional regulation, and the knowledge that this is their job, and they can succeed no matter what the obstacles. If you don't feel all those things today, they can be learned and enhanced over time with practice. Having a pool of supporters and advisors can help. I had a colleague who used to routinely tell me "You can cope, Valerie, you can cope." It always made me laugh and that helped, maybe not as much as having contingency plans, but it helped!

BOUNCING FORWARD

Nothing is achieved without embracing the risk of learning.

—TODD DEWETT

In the end, knowing that there are lessons to be learned can help get you through the tough times. It helps to know that today's adversity is tomorrow's knowledge and strength. It's okay to rely on platitudes in bad times. Also, you should remember that you're not the first project manager who has struggled or felt hopeless. If you can find a peer or coach who has been there before you, they will assure you that you are not alone.

Thomas Koslowski and Patricia Longstaff believe that acquiring resilience isn't just the ability to bounce back; rather, the goal should be to bounce forward. Bouncing forward means you're coming back stronger and are better positioned to move successfully into the future. If you're lucky, you will find that you won't just bounce back from adversity during your project, but will cultivate effort to bounce forward by responding to the actual situation in front of you, not the one you wish was happening. As Karen Ferris says, "When we bounce forward, we learn from the experience and are better for it."

REFERENCES

Aldrich, Rebekkah Smith. *Resilience.* Chicago: American Library Association, 2018.

Allison-Napolitano, Elle. *Bounce Forward: The Extraordinary Resilience of Leadership.* Thousand Oaks, CA: Corwin, 2014.

American Library Association. "Resilience." https://www.ala.org/tools/future/trends/resilience.

Brown, Brené. *Rising Strong: How the Ability to Reset Transforms the Way We Live, Love, Parent, and Lead.* New York: Random House, 2017.

Dyer, Jeff, Hal B. Gregersen, and Clayton M. Christensen. *The Innovator's DNA: Mastering the Five Skills of Disruptive Innovators.* Boston: Harvard Business Review Press, 2011.

Gates, Bill. "Bill Gates: My Plan to Fix the World's Biggest Problems—Measure Them!" *Wall Street Journal,* January 26, 2013.

Kawasaki, Guy Takeo. *The Top 10 Mistakes of Entrepreneurs*. YouTube video, March 11, 2013.

Koslowski, Thomas G., and Patricia H. Longstaff. "Resilience Undefined: A Framework for Interdisciplinary Communication and Application to Real-World Problems." In *Disaster Management: Enabling Resilience*, 3–20. Cham, Switz.: Springer International, 2014.

Masten, A., K. Best, and N. Garmezy. "Resilience and Development: Contributions from the Study of Children Who Overcome Adversity." *Development and Psychopathology* 2 (1990): 425–44.

Seligman, Martin E. P. *Learned Optimism*. New York: Alfred A. Knopf, 1991.

Tough, Paul. *How Children Succeed: Grit, Curiosity, and the Hidden Power of Character*. Boston: Houghton Mifflin Harcourt, 2012.

Waters, Richard. "The Exclusive Interview with Bill Gates," *Financial Times Magazine*, November 1, 2013.

THREE

INNOVATION
A Discovery Process

THE ART OF DISCOVERY

Cooperation is part of the professional DNA of research librarians, and innovation must increasingly be viewed not just at the local level, but in the context of new collaborations at national and global systematic strategies.

—JAMES G. NEAL

There are two fundamental actions or practices you need to embrace in order to be successful working at a large scale—innovation and collaboration. This chapter looks at innovation, and the next chapter examines collaboration. To work at scale, you need to understand the theoretical underpinnings behind both concepts. Both activities should be built into project design, and it will help you justify your initiative if you have an articulated case to make for innovation and collaboration.

What is innovation? The standard definition from the *Oxford English Dictionary* (OED) calls innovation the act of moving away from established forms to new ones. Yawn. Ronald C. Jantz defines innovation as introducing a new product, service, or technology, or an improvement to an existing product, service, or practice. True enough. I think of innovation as something that has an impact or a *wow* factor, but mostly I see it as an active process of discovery. Another way of thinking of innovation is as a professional norm that includes specific actions that should be taken by all librarians.

It's interesting to note that the *OED* definition does not use the terms *invention* or *creativity* in defining innovation. Creativity, according to the best-selling author David Burkus, is the generation of novel and useful ideas, so it can be thought of as the genesis of innovation. You can't have innovation without creativity, but without taking innovative action, creativity is just a nice idea.

Innovation, as I will use it, is the process of pushing boundaries, taking risks, and exploring opportunities, all to have an impact. Libraries and library staff should adopt a philosophy of innovation, much as they adopt one of customer service. Ask yourself the following questions:

- Do you see innovation as part of your core job function?
- Is it your job to bring new ideas into your library?
- Do you scan for trends and other exciting opportunities occurring in our field or in other fields that could improve your library?
- Are there unexplored ways of doing your work better?

Innovation should be part of every professional's toolkit. While librarians have always honored our traditions, we have never hesitated to improve our practices or offer new services. Has there ever been a time when we need to have innovative libraries more than now?

TELL ME AGAIN, WHY I SHOULD CARE?

We [librarians] are a society and a field, addicted to innovation.

—R. DAVID LANKES

Do you see innovation as a tool or as a value? Innovation can be considered a tool to achieve a goal. It can also be a value that needs to be built into the bedrock of a library's work culture. How you define innovation will impact how you learn about it and how you act upon it. As I mentioned, my definition of innovation is that it is an active process of discovery. I lean toward treating innovation as a value so I can build motivation, discovery, and risk-taking into the culture of the organizations I managed. This is not easy to do, but it is a worthwhile goal to aspire to.

Like many terms, innovation can be overused to the point of blandness. But many of the concepts that compose innovative actions have merit on their own:

- Adaptations
- Challenging norms
- Looking for trends and new concepts
- Identifying unanticipated needs
- Rewarding creativity
- Accepting risks and embracing failure
- Flexibility
- Experimentation

By adopting principles like trend-watching, experimentation, welcoming risk, and reframing failure as a learning opportunity, we can bring innovation into our libraries.

When business experts write about innovation, they laud its ability to improve productivity, reduce costs, bring more competitive advantages, improve public perceptions, help establish stakeholder relationships, and improve staff morale while decreasing turnover. That is a lot to expect from innovation, but in my experience much of it is true, especially the ability to improve customer services and enhance the reputation of the library within its community.

Business pundits also cite the enormous costs of *not* innovating; just look at the cost of maintaining the status quo at Blockbuster, Kodak, or Radio Shack. Libraries must constantly fight to challenge a stodgy reputation; nothing challenges that notion more than innovation.

Colorado's Anythink libraries (Rangeview Library District) were struggling when the new director, Pam Sandlian Smith, came in. She told me they had nothing to lose, and so she reinvented their entire library system, going from a poorly funded and seldom-used library system to one that has won just about every library award available. Anythink's vision states that they are "the catalyst for innovation in our community." You can read more about Smith's process of reinventing libraries in her 2011 article "Managing Innovation: Creating Anythink."

We live in times when public dollars are tightening, the pandemic is raging, and being perceived as stodgy will not increase our funding base.

Furthermore, we face fierce competition in a way we didn't have thirty years ago. Dozens of undergraduate surveys have found that students claim they find research material on the internet; they don't say they found their research information on the internet through the library. Reinvention is a viable path forward if the status quo is under severe strain. Ronald C. Jantz did a study of Association of Research Libraries (ARL) deans in 2011. Jantz said that every dean he interviewed believed innovation was crucial to the future of their library system. Each of those deans believed that innovation was growing in importance, and they were all actively looking for ways to incorporate more experimentation and risk-taking into their core work processes.

Public libraries are the same as illustrated by Carolyn A. Anthony, the 2014 president of the Public Library Association, who has argued that the very future of public libraries depends on continuous innovation. Anthony believes that the route to innovate in public libraries is outward toward the community. Kirstie Nicholson's delightful book *Innovation in Public Libraries* is filled with examples of public libraries that have pushed the envelope. She says in the book: "It is this willingness and enthusiasm to invent, experiment and innovate that ensures that public libraries will continue to be relevant and valued community institutions far into the future."

In his influential work *Diffusion of Innovations*, Everett Rogers researched how well innovation was accepted within organizations. He argues that the critical element of innovation acceptance is whether the new product is perceived as being better than whatever it is replacing. He found that the alignment between the new product and the perception of how consistent that product is with the core values and culture of the organization is also important. Rogers's thesis is crucial to why we want to engage in innovative activities. It is all about perceptions, alignment, and the genuine belief that there is an advantage to libraries in bringing in new or improved services or products. As you go forward with a large-scale initiative, it is important to never lose sight of the power of perception. You should get used to saying, this project will make it better!

Innovation is there to be adopted by everyone who works in a library. We all need to adopt actions like trend-watching, experimentation, welcoming risk, and redefining failure. We need to continue to send a clear message to the community about our commitment to remaining inventive and relevant.

THE TAXONOMY OF INNOVATION

Innovation can be a disruption or incremental and sustaining.

—ANTHONY MOLARO ET AL.

Researchers like Clayton Christensen have identified two ways that innovation can be adopted: the core innovation model and the new growth model. The *core innovation model* involves taking today's product or service and improving or enhancing it incrementally. Think about library catalogs. Back in the mid-1980s, the first online catalog I worked on reproduced the circle from the bottom of the catalog card because that's how the print card catalog systems worked. Today's new intuitive, language-based online catalogs are the product of decades of slow, incremental improvements.

By contrast, the *new growth model* involves creating a new product, pushing into new markets, or developing a new business model. This model can be disruptive. You may be identifying a need that doesn't exist today but will eventually become an invaluable service to users. It seemed like it took only a blink of the eye and suddenly libraries were offering coding classes in their state-of-the-art makerspaces.

Ronald Jantz's study of ARL deans found that they were all committed to incremental innovation. ARL libraries have substantial infrastructure embedded in the support of existing service models. It makes sense that their deans talk about "adopting ongoing, incremental improvements," or "bringing different concepts and services together to provide innovative customer service." Furthermore, the deans told Jantz, they were most interested in seeing what other schools were doing and synthesizing those developments. One dean described this as being "committed fast-followers" and proclaimed that they evaluated the work of others before implementing anything new.

Christina Wandi's 2019 Copenhagen study followed public libraries for five years and identified seven factors needed to bring about transformational change. These factors include creating value for patrons, setting change-related targets, preparing staff for the changes to come, building staff skills, and collaborating outside of the library. After years of research, Wandi concluded that transformational change was extremely difficult. In fact, her conclusion stated that transformational change wouldn't happen fast and takes patience and time. How that differs from incremental change is beyond me.

There are examples of libraries launching new, transformational services. I worked with one in the early 1990s. I was the information technology head for a large academic library, and our peers were bringing in CD-ROM towers to provide access to periodical literature. We chose to jump over that step, purchased periodical indexes directly from the vendor, and tape-loaded the article-level records directly into our online catalog. This approach was ahead of its time by fifteen years. It was a bumpy process compared to the integration of periodical literature and books found in today's catalogs. However, in choosing to take the risk of bypassing a stage of technology development, we provided our students and faculty with vastly more information from one source. It was time-consuming and more expensive, but it had a huge payoff in better access for the library's patrons.

As discussed in the last chapter, Guy Kawasaki argues that the ability to jump ahead of the curve is crucial to creating a new product or service that revolutionizes how our work is done. Whether you favor incremental innovation or are a believer in the jump-ahead model, you should be paying attention to which path you select. You'll want to use the tools that fit either an incremental approach or the more radical jump-ahead approach. Many decisions will follow from the path you choose, ranging from how you promote your project, to the technology you use to implement it. In my experience, the key is to keep the goal of improving service to patrons and library staff at the forefront, no matter which path you use to get there.

INNOVATION IS A STATE OF MIND

Everybody can be an innovator, as long as you really want to.

—GIJS VAN WULFEN

There is an array of tools, techniques, and mindsets you can learn to help you innovate. The next sections will look specifically at those items. I have found in a wide variety of conversations about innovation that everyone has a personal innovation belief structure that covers the gamut from "let's jump in and see what happens" to "wait for the other guy to go first." Research has shown us that there are traits associated with those more comfortable pushing the envelope.

Gijs van Wulfen in *The Innovation Expedition* created a five-question test to help you judge your innovation mindset. Do you:

1. Want to move forward or progress in life.
2. Be open to the world around you.
3. Continuously gain fresh insights.
4. See opportunities and develop new ideas.
5. Put effort into realizing your new ideas.

The higher you rate yourself on these five questions, the more likely you are to use innovative techniques in your professional work.

The Psychology of Creativity

The most important thing is that creative people know how to adapt to different situations.

—JANJA POPOVIĆ

The question of why some people seem more creative than others has been the subject of many studies. Having a foundation in this theoretical model can help as you prepare to move into the ideation stage of your project. Keep in mind that we are defining creativity as coming up with new ideas, and innovation as the action of implementing those new ideas. Creativity requires the ability to ponder the what-if, while innovation requires the ability to put that what-if into action.

Over decades of research, there is remarkable unanimity on what types of personalities are most likely to embrace creativity as a tool. It turns out there is a creative-type person. Researchers like Silvia Da Costa have found that inventive people behave differently from people who display less inventiveness. These studies often use the five-factor psychological model as their frame of reference. The common factors found in creative people are:

- More autonomous (self-governance, independent, nonconforming)
- Extroversion (outgoing, assertive, energetic)
- Open to new experiences
- Willing to push boundaries
- Dominant (status-oriented, influential, controlling)
- Hostile (mistrust and confrontational attitudes)
- Impulsivity (urgency, perseverance, sensation-seeking)

These factors are on a sliding scale and are not static. You may like to go bungee-jumping in your spare time while preferring cautious incremental change at work. We all fall somewhere along the continuum, and we move along that continuum in different situations and as we learn new skills.

Creative people have countless ways of demonstrating the imaginative traits. One notable metric looked at the differences in how willing people were to be in social settings, and their verbal dexterity in wooing people with their ideas. Think of inventors like Steve Jobs or Elon Musk who have strong, often abrasive personalities, but who can also woo major investors, star employees, and TED Talk enthusiasts to their cause. Other creative people prefer to work out of the bright lights but want to push the needle in their field of expertise.

So how do we enhance our creativity? Many writers and speakers have tried to distill the creative juices into traits and skills that can be taught or enhanced. Books on creativity are often in the best-seller category. For example, David Kelley's *Creative Confidence* has been well-reviewed. Most writers on creativity, however, do not see it as a single attribute, but instead as a combination of traits and behaviors that blend together to build ingenuity. As you go forward with working on large-scale initiatives, you might want to consider your skills as related to the following creative traits. Creative traits include:

1. *Openness*: This denotes a high willingness to accept change, coupled with a belief that change can make the situation better than it currently is. Another trait is being open to diverse collaborations that allow an exchange of ideas while working toward a shared goal.
2. *Divergent thinking*: Having divergent thinking skills means that you can generate numerous ideas when faced with a problem, have the ability to switch between perspectives with some ease, and possess the ability to find new associations between things that may not appear to be similar. The opposite is convergent thinking, or aiming for a single, correct solution to a problem. Divergence is the home base of *what-if* thinking.
3. *Self-assurance*: Creative people often possess a higher than average sense of their self-worth and have a well-developed personal awareness. They can be intellectuals, great leaders, or creative artists (think George Patton, Joan Crawford, or Steven Jobs).

4. *Problem-solving skills*: This trait includes the ability to recognize a problem or identify a unique, unexpected need. It often involves dismissing the common solution, asking the unexpected question, or going for that remarkable idea that surprises and brings about significant change.
5. *Playfulness and flexibility*: There is biological evidence that humor stimulates the creativity parts of the brain and improves performance on creative tasks. Adaptive flexibility is described as the ability to look for a novel solution to a situation. It involves the ability to give up the first, simple solution presented and seek a more nuanced way of addressing the problem.
6. *Decision-making*: The ability to use judgment and discretion to refine ideas is part of creative decision-making. Finding the appropriate solution includes the ability to know when to follow the crowd, and when to break out from the norms.
7. *Communication*: This involves using a variety of communication skills (verbal, visual, and kinesthetic) to get your point across to a broad set of listeners. It also entails the confidence to express authentic feelings and beliefs across a variety of social mediums. If a creative idea upsets the status quo, does the communicator have the confidence to defend their idea?

This list can help you evaluate and work effectively with your project team members. In reading this list, you will see areas of overlap among the traits within your team. Finally, these traits must be coupled with the ability to take decisive action, to move out of the ideation stage into the implementation stage. That requires self-regulation, ambition, drive, and achievement-orientation.

Creative Organizations

Challenging assumptions is key to innovation . . . At Anythink, we focus on the interactions between people and information . . . that surprise, delight, and inspire curiosity.

—PAM SANDLIAN SMITH

Like people, libraries can be innovative. But for an organization to move away from focusing on the traditional often takes strong, visionary leadership. We can identify many cases where libraries took the jump and went for transformational change. Back in the 1990s, Carla Stoffle brought in the then-radical concept of team management to the University of Arizona (UA) Libraries. For the first few years of her tenure, every library position advertised in New Mexico attracted numerous UA Libraries applicants who were looking to change jobs. I visited the UA Libraries five or six years into the team management transition, and Stoffle told me that it had taken years longer than she'd anticipated, but she felt they had gained the payoff from the radical new system she had introduced. You can read about the revolutionary changes that took place at the UA Libraries in Stoffle's "Choosing Our Futures" article in *College and Research Libraries*.

Why do some libraries like Rangeview's Anythink or the University of Arizona decide to jump off the incremental path of innovation and adopt radical transformation? Why are they so different from the ARL dean's incrementalism as found in Jantz's interviews? What factors made the people in one organization more willing to change than those in another? There is research on this from outside the library field that can be applied to libraries.

Organizations can adopt behaviors that foster creativity and innovation. Back in 1926, Graham Wallas identified four steps in the creative process: preparation, incubation, illumination, and verification. Decades later, Runco et al. expanded the steps to six:

1. *Orientation*: This is a time of interest, avid curiosity, and significant information-gathering.
2. *Incubation*: Defining the problem, looking at the situation from new angles, diving into ideation. The focus is on staying open to new inputs. This is a time to step back and let your mind wander. Research shows that allowing an idea to lay fallow can be an effective strategy before jumping into action.
3. *Illumination*: This step involves divergent thinking, openness, and excitement. This is that eureka moment that gets so much press but is actually the accumulated input from many previous steps, and from encountering many other diverse thinkers or ideas.

4. *Verification*: This step involves comparison to other work, and deep explorations of the idea. This is a step where your idea is built upon, analyzed, and evaluated, and this question is asked: is this truly a useful and novel solution?
5. *Communication*: This involves testing the idea in the wider arena, and seeking expert opinions. In this step, you are polishing your message and testing your ideas and initial plans.
6. *Validation*: This involves going public and seeking social acceptance of the idea. You're going for buy-in, support, and information networks that will allow your idea to expand.

This model may be worth sharing with your steering committee. You can chart where you are as you build toward your ideation process.

EXPERIMENTATION: A BIG DEAL GETS BIGGER

Failure and invention are inseparable twins.

—JEFF BEZOS

Figuring out how to foster innovation can cause anxiety for both managers and project funders. Our culture holds a widespread belief that innovation is a quintessential American value, but that belief comes with a boatload of uncertainty. In his book *Experimentation Works,* Stefan Thomke recommends using the scientific method as part of your innovation process in order to lessen uncertainty. The idea here is to follow the familiar scientific method in your decision-making. The three steps Thomke recommends are:

1. Generate a testable hypothesis.
2. Run an experiment with a control group.
3. Learn from the experiment's success or failure.

You can test out the results of your innovative experiment. For example, if you want to launch a new logo, develop your logo while retaining your current one. Next, test out the new logo with focus groups before going live with the new design. Finally, learn from the reaction.

Thomke sees this method playing out in all businesses, but it has the strongest footprint in the digital world. Given that libraries rely heavily on their digital presence, there is much to learn from this model. Thomke believes that large-scale, controlled experimentation could revolutionize how we make decisions. However, we should be aware that research shows that experiments often have a high failure rate, reaching as high as 90 percent. Thomke's case studies demonstrate that everyone is terrible at predicting the behavior of others. He doesn't see these high failure rates as a problem, though, because even a failed test teaches an organization how to improve.

While Thomke is speaking about organizational culture changes, his work also applies to large-scale initiatives. A project will develop a culture of its own that can be separated from the parent organization sponsoring the project. If the initiative eventually breaks away from the parent organization, it can take that culture with it. Starting your project with a commitment to experimentation as part of the design can impact not just your current work, but potentially the future success of your endeavor.

ACCEPTING FAILURE

If you aren't failing, you aren't trying hard enough.

—JOHN HELMER

John Helmer, formerly of Orbis Cascade Alliance, often talked about how our profession is hesitant to take risks and start new projects, as well as shut down outdated or poor-performing systems. He argues that we need to permit ourselves to fail, and in fact, we need to fail to allow us to let go of no-longer-needed services or outmoded ways of thinking.

Failure is simply being unsuccessful or falling short of your goals. Those are simple words that we overlay with a great deal of meaning. In building an environment for experimentation, accepting failure should be a part of the landscape. I'm often struck in talking to people how much more we learn from people who are willing to be up-front about their failures. Libraries should be both incubators of success and admirers of good-hearted attempts that fail.

A few years ago, an entrepreneurial-focused business movement called "fail fast" sprang up in the computer programming arena, and was popularized in Babineaux and Krumboltz's book *Fail Fast, Fail Often*. The book is associated with the lean start-up movement as laid out by Eric Ries in his 2011 book. These authors argue that the goal isn't necessarily to fail but to put an idea out there and test to see if it works, and then learn from its success or failure.

This method is seen as a way of marshalling resources, proving your project concept, and redirecting work away from unusable paths early in project development. If you design your project plan with speed as part of the infrastructure, you can allocate your resources early on to test your hypothesis about your new library product. By chunking the work plan, you can stay agile in shifting resources around as you continue to move toward your goal. There are also benefits from having a smaller-scale prototype fail when the consequences can be kept manageable. Think of this as taking risks on the cheap.

Libraries can't afford to put a massive amount of resources into a project, take years to build it, launch it with fanfare, and then find that it doesn't work. It is far better to launch small pieces of your project and see how they perform first. To fail fast, you first need to make sure that your experiment's scope is clearly defined. You also need to make sure that you have defined what success is for your experiment before you launch it. Finally, you need to announce through a big megaphone that this is a test, or a pilot, or some other wording that alerts people to the experimental nature of your product release.

It's a truism that failure is a better teacher than success. With 25 percent of start-up companies failing in their first year and 71 percent by their tenth year, we can assume there is a lot of learning going on. Research published in 2010 by Madsen and Desai found, after analyzing disasters like NASA's *Challenger* explosion, that organizations learn better from failure than from success, and the larger the failure, the bigger the impact from the lessons learned. Large-scale failure can catapult an organization into embracing a learning-based culture.

Failure has been found to inspire creativity as well. There is nothing like failure to disrupt the old procedures and services that can bog a library down. Failure can cause organizations to reinvent and redefine themselves going forward. This holds for large-scale project work as well. If you are working at a large scale, there will be many steps in the process, and some will not work well. If before you start, you commit to treating all those unsuccessful efforts as learning opportunities, you might ensure greater success overall.

Concepts like fail fast and *agility* are often dismissed as merely the latest buzzwords in business. Agility is tied to software development and is associated with iterative, incremental, and evolutionary development. The agility movement pushes for the fast delivery of the product, constant improvement, a flexible approach, and a commitment to checking in with the users of the software. These methods are not without criticism, which is often centered around the negativity of failing. The *Wikipedia* entry on "Agile Software Development" lists an astonishing fifteen major concerns for companies using the process. In a similar vein, the "fail fast" concept has been criticized for being all hype and no substance.

I think these criticisms are mostly legitimate, but so is what the fail-fast community is trying to achieve. Libraries have *traditionally* been very *traditional* organizations. To open up space for creativity and for pushing the borders of what is acceptable and even imaginable within the library sphere, I believe concepts like fail fast can help pry open minds to the willingness to take risks. You don't have to use the terminology of the fail-fast business culture, but you can use its concepts in your push to make your initiative truly innovative and impactful.

INNOVATION AS A PANACEA? WELL, MAYBE NOT

Courage is a skill.

—KATHLEEN REARDON

As I've written this chapter, I have tried to highlight some of the downsides of innovation. However, there are some unique risks with a publicly funded organization like a library adopting innovative practices, and these deserve further consideration. Libraries are all about efficiencies; this is one of our deepest professional norms. We always strive to be good stewards of public funds. There are times when taking a risk and doing something big with the potential to fail can feel like it pushes too hard against our traditionally self-preserving norms.

Perhaps things have changed, but when I went to library school, no one told me that part of my professional duties was to bring new ideas into my organization. If you read the ALA's Code of Ethics, there is no mention that librarians will push the envelope to bring new, novel, inspiring services to their patrons. This confuses me: why aren't creativity, innovation, and risk-taking seen as core imperatives in libraries?

Furthermore, many people who work in libraries are afraid that if they do something that carries a risk of spectacular failure, they will ruin their professional reputation, or at least their social status with their library colleagues. This fear of loss of prestige is no small matter and has probably stopped more innovation from occurring inside libraries than any other single factor.

The counterargument to this kind of thinking is from Clayton Christensen's work. If you don't adopt and change, in a society like ours where rapid disruption is the new norm, you can easily become outdated and cease to exist. In trying to keep our modest status quo, we can be our own worst enemy.

TWIN SONS OF DIFFERENT MOTHERS

Innovation requires bravery, which is not the opposite of cowardice. The opposite of bravery is conformity.

—PHIL McKINNEY

Not everyone dares to be disruptively innovative. In my experience, most libraries readily embrace incremental improvements, and Ronald Thomke's work with ARL deans found that to be true. Within large-scale library initiatives, you might well have a project that lends itself to incremental change, and if so, you are lucky.

But if you are trying to do something remarkable and transformational, you probably will be on the disruptive innovation path, and then you will meet resistance from several sources. The pushback you receive will not be called fear of change or fear of failure—but that is likely to be the underlying cause of any negative feedback you get from within the profession.

There are several things you can do to prepare for the pushback generated by launching an innovative project. Having a great elevator speech ready can help. Quoting experts like Clayton Christensen on disruptive innovation and the fate of companies like Blockbuster and Radio Shack can help. But the real secret to making disruptive innovation work in libraries lies with innovation's kissing cousin—collaboration. The next chapter looks at collaboration in detail.

REFERENCES

American Library Association. "Professional Ethics." www.ala.org/tools/ethics.

Anthony, Carolyn A. 2014. "Innovation in Public Libraries." *Public Libraries* 53 (2014): 5–7.

Babineaux, Ryan, and John Krumboltz. *Fail Fast, Fail Often: How Losing Can Help You Win.* Jeremy P. Tarcher/Penguin, 2014.

Catmull, Ed. *Creativity, Inc.* Corgi, 2015.

Christensen, Clayton M. *The Innovator's Dilemma: The Revolutionary Book That Will Change the Way You Do Business.* New York: Harper Business, 2011.

Costa, Silvia Da, Darío Páez, Flor Sánchez, Maite Garaigordobil, and Sonia Gondim. "Personal Factors of Creativity: A Second Order Meta-Analysis." *Revista de Psicología del Trabajo y de las Organizaciones* 31 (2015): 165–73.

Feist, Gregory J. "A Meta-Analysis of Personality in Scientific and Artistic Creativity." *Personality and Social Psychology Review* 2 (2016): 290–309.

Helmer, John F. and Horton, Valerie. "Finding Joy in Our Profession: John F. Helmer on Library Consortia," *Collaborative Librarianship* 7 (2015).

Jantz, Ronald C. "Innovation in Academic Libraries: An Analysis of University Librarians' Perspectives." *Library and Information Science Research* 34 (2012): 3–12.

———. *Managing Creativity: The Innovative Research Library.* ACRL Publications in Librarianship, No. 70. Chicago: Association of College and Research Libraries, 2016.

Kelley, David, and Tom Kelley. *Creative Confidence: Unleashing the Creative Potential within Us All.* New York: Crown Business, 2013.

Koestler, Arthur. *The Act of Creation.* New York: Macmillan, 1965.

Madsen, Peter M., and Vinit Desai. "Failing to Learn? The Effects of Failure and Success on Organizational Learning in the Global Orbital Launch Vehicle Industry." *Academy of Management Journal* 53 (2010): 451.

Nicholson, Kirstie. *Innovation in Public Libraries.* Cambridge, MA: Chandos, 2017.

Ries, Eric. *The Lean Startup: How Constant Innovation Creates Radically Successful Businesses.* London: Portfolio Penguin, 2011.

Rogers, Everett M. *Diffusion of Innovations.* 5th ed. New York: Free Press, 2003.

Runco, Pritzker, Mark A. Runco, and Steven R. Pritzker. *Encyclopedia of Creativity.* 2nd ed. Boston: Elsevier, 2011.

Smith, Pam Sandlian. "Managing Innovation: Creating Anythink." *Journal of Library Innovation* 2 (2011): 5–7.

Sternberg, Robert J., and Todd I. Lubart. *Defying the Crowd: Cultivating Creativity in a Culture of Conformity.* New York: Free Press, 1995.

Stoddard, Morgan M., Bill Gillis, and Peter Cohn. "Agile Project Management in Libraries: Creating Collaborative, Resilient, Responsive Organizations." *Journal of Library Administration* 59 (2019): 492–511.

Stoffle, Carla J., Robert Renaud, and Jerilyn R. Veldof. "Choosing Our Futures." *College & Research Libraries* 57 (1996): 213–33.

Thomke, Stefan. *Experimentation Works: The Surprising Power of Business Experiments.* Harvard Business Review Press, 2020.

Utterback, James M. *Mastering the Dynamics of Innovation: How Companies Can Seize Opportunities in the Face of Technological Change.* Boston: Harvard Business School Press, 1994.

Van Wulfen, Gijs. *The Innovation Expedition: A Visual Toolkit to Start Innovation.* Amsterdam: BIS, 2014.

Wandi, Christina. "Change Management in Public Libraries: Seven Recommendations from Copenhagen Libraries." *Journal of Library Administration* 59 (2019): 915–26.

FOUR

COLLABORATION
An Unnatural Act

AN UNNATURAL ACT

Library cooperation is an unnatural act.

—WARD SHAW

Most people think of collaboration as a soft skill and dismiss it with an "Oh yeah, that's nice" shrug. Here's the thing, though: you don't collaborate to make people feel okay, you don't collaborate because it's expected of you, and you don't collaborate to earn brownie points—you collaborate because on large-scale projects you have no choice. It is a necessity.

Library staff have always seen the value of cooperation. Adrian Alexander claimed that we've been cooperating since the first professional librarian was trained in America. I am a believer, along with Ward Shaw, in the unnatural act of collaboration. I was one of the founding editors of the journal *Collaborative Librarianship*, have published two books and more than ten articles on the topic, and have served as the director of two library consortia. I have the credentials to say that collaboration is difficult, but without even more collaboration in the future, libraries will not thrive. William Jordan was even blunter when he said, "Libraries have a choice; we can collaborate, or we can die."

I conducted an informal survey and found that a typical large academic library had around 15–25 collaborative partners, while a large public library had about half that number. The Georgetown University Library is a case in point. The Georgetown library has roughly twenty partners, including large national organizations (HathiTrust), a regional consortium (the Northeast Research Library Consortium), campus partners (writing center), and the local coffee shop. The Denver Public Library lists twelve local partners, including the *Denver Post*, the Colorado Library Consortium, and the Tattered Cover Bookstore.

Librarians must do hard things, and collaboration is one of them. George Machovec, director of the Colorado Alliance of Research Libraries, has spoken about how collaboration is key to what libraries do. He lists more than a dozen areas where librarians actively collaborate, from print volume storage to shared catalogs, to resource-sharing. Despite the length of his list, I've often wondered how deeply collaboration has infiltrated into libraries' DNA. This chapter will look at research and best practices regarding collaboration and how to apply these findings and lessons learned to your large-scale initiative.

AM I COLLABORATING, COOPERATING, OR WHAT?

The power of collaboration comes from inclusion.

—DAVID STRAUS

It turns out that librarians care a lot about definitions. There are differences between the words teamwork, cooperation, partnerships, collaboration, and deep collaboration. It's best to reach agreement on how you will be using terminology early in your project development. Dictionaries define *cooperation* as a situation in which people agree to work together, while *collaboration* is a more formal term that is used for work between two people or a group to achieve specific results.

In 2012, Wheeler and Hilton researched the topic and found that the term *collaboration* was used most often to imply a greater level of engagement. In 2008, the Ohio State University Libraries developed a good definition: "Collaboration is two or more people or organizations combining their resources and working together to achieve a common and mutually beneficial goal." While there are differences between collaboration and cooperation, I will be using both words interchangeably throughout this book. After all, Montiel-Overall defined *cooperation* and *collaboration* as ubiquitous terms whose meanings vary across different professional and academic disciplines.

In libraries, collaborations share some basic characteristics, including:

- clearly defined and agreed-upon vision and goals
- high levels of engagement and time commitments
- intensive use of information resources and staff expertise
- willingness to adapt and change local processes as the work progresses
- reciprocity coupled with negotiation and compromise
- congeniality, information-sharing, and dialogue
- and, most importantly, shared power and decision-making

Most writers on the topic see collaboration existing on a continuum from casual effort to profound, integrated commitments. Wheeler and Hilton describe deep and effective collaboration as concentrating on shared and actively pursued objectives. They warn against both passive and unbalanced cooperative efforts. With unbalanced collaboration, resource commitment and expectations are not aligned among participants. Their main point is that effective collaboration requires constant attention and an intense focus on goals. Working from these considerations, I published a definition of deep collaboration in 2013, derived from the Ohio State definition: "Deep Collaboration is two or more people or organizations contributing substantial levels of personal or organizational commitment, including shared authority, joint responsibility, and robust resources allocation, to achieve a common or mutually beneficial goal."

To make a large-scale library project successful, you will need to consider how deep your collaborative efforts should go. It has been my experience as a project manager that you will spend as much time dealing with your partners as you do with the actual day-to-day work of your project. It's best to have a common language going into any joint effort and decide what type of buy-in you need from each type of participating organization.

WHY BOTHER?

Collaboration is a logical path in austere times.

—REBECCA GAJDA

As with innovation, there are many reasons why libraries choose to collaborate. Most decisions to cooperate come down to two core motivations:

1. *Lower cost*: Gary Lawrence argues that stand-alone institutions, even the biggest, are still too small to effectively compete in today's vendor marketplace.
2. *Better services*: The second reason is to improve the services and information resources available to patrons or staff. Lorcan Dempsey summarized this motivation as a way "to improve the impact and efficiency of their services, and increasingly to accelerate learning and innovation in a complex environment."

There are a host of other reasons to work together, but these two reasons dominate library discussions. The fundamental question a library director will ask about a collaborative project is: can we save money, *and* can we improve resources and services to our patrons?

Second-tier reasons to collaborate include the advantages gained by working with others and getting more input from wider perspectives, knowledge, and working environments. The broader your expertise and experiences, the richer the inputs will be that guide the development of your initiative. Among other advantages of collaboration are improved efficiency and streamlined workflows, especially if services (think cataloging or delivery) can be done externally by consortium staff. George Needham has said, "there's simply no excuse anymore for duplicating work among libraries. Anything that can be done collaboratively should be done." In this argument, libraries would have as few in-house technical services staff as possible. The goal is to free up as much staff time as possible for direct patron and community engagement.

Collaborations can help change the reputation of libraries from that of stodgy 1970s navel-gazing organizations to active participants in their communities. The simple reality is that collaborative initiatives are viewed by most as more important, more appealing, and more career-enhancing. It is prestigious and educational to be involved with Measures that Matter or the Library Publishing Coalition.

COLLABORATION MODELS

Collaborative innovation is not a single approach, but takes a wide variety of forms.

—GARY PISANO AND ROBERTO VERGANTI

Pisano and Verganti have identified four collaboration models. Their framework allows managers to determine how their projects should be organized based on key metrics. To determine which collaboration model to select, you need to ask those in authority two foundational questions.

- How open or closed will our project be to potential partners?
- Who will have final decision-making authority on the project?

Regarding the first question, think about crowdsourcing projects: they are open to anyone who finds the proposal online. This openness contrasts with a typical library consortium, which has clearly defined criteria for membership.

Pisano and Verganti's four models use a matrix based on whether your project is open or closed to new members and outside input, and whether the project is flat (all partners have equal decision-making authority) or hierarchical (decision-making is bureaucratic and controlled). The four models are:

1. *Elite circle*: a closed and hierarchical network. One entity selects the members, defines the problem, and implements the solution.
2. *Innovation mall*: an open and hierarchical network. One entity proposes a problem, but anyone can propose solutions, with the originating entity choosing the best solution.
3. *Innovation community*: an open and flat network. Anyone can post a problem, many can offer solutions, and the group decides which solution to implement.
4. *Consortium*: a closed and flat network. A tightly defined group of participants sets up a complex organization to decide which problems to solve, choose who will do the work, and implement the solution.

These four models of collaboration come with different trade-offs, according to Pisano and Verganti. The model you select will be the one that best matches your project. For instance, do you need additional financial, labor, or physical resources to make the project work? If so, you will probably need additional partners, and that may mean you will have to allow more sharing of authority and decision-making. In contrast, if you don't need help from others, you can keep all the autonomy and control you want. The trade-off with collaboration is typically between participation/sharing and autonomy/control.

When considering these options, Pisano and Verganti argue that closed networks tend to be smaller and harder to join. An academic-only library consortium like Orbis Cascade has a predetermined geographic service area that limits its membership growth. Open networks tend to be larger and easier to join, with most potential contributors being unknown to each other. An open-source library software catalog, like Koha, can have numerous libraries downloading the software, but it also has a core group of developers who form user groups, make financial commitments, and put limits on who can develop the software. All these decisions are on a sliding scale. Pisano and Verganti argue that the quality of potential partners lessens as you move from a closed network to an open one.

Flat or hierarchical governance structures determine who defines the problem and who gets to say when the right solution is found. A flat governance model, like the National Information Standards Organization (NISO), has a set governance structure that determines which standards will be developed and adopted. The larger participant community might help with developing a new standard but is not part of the final decision-making. In a hierarchical structure, there tends to be specific expertise or authority that is recognized by participants and accepted in making decisions. NISO pays close attention to experts in the field when standards are being developed.

All of these approaches work, but you need to have a clear understanding of the structure that you will be operating within. By knowing your organizational structure, you can focus on the strength of that model and make necessary trade-offs that advance your goals. As Pisano and Verganti state, "To stay ahead in the race to develop new technologies, designs, and services, companies must revisit their approach to collaborative innovation as their strategies evolve."

EXERCISING THE COLLABORATIVE MUSCLE

Collaboration is a muscle; the more it is used, the stronger it gets.

—MICHAEL RIDLEY

What can you do to make the collaborative part of your project work better? Researchers have been studying the best techniques to help project managers. This section includes examples of tools and techniques you can adopt to make your large-scale initiative more successful.

The vision thing. I'm starting this section with the importance of having a compelling vision, because experts identify those who are guided by high-level aspirations as better able to overcome difficulties and be successful overall. Your vision guides you into the future and helps you stay focused on what is important while keeping you aligned with your mission and goals. It is easy to get lost in the day-to-day grind of project details; holding your vision front and center requires effort but pays off. A large longitudinal study by Claudine Gartenberg et al. found that better performance occurs in endeavors whose participants have a strong belief in the project's purpose, and there is clarity from management about that purpose.

Vision statements are inspirational and idealistic and often touch on emotions which can make some librarians uncomfortable. It is no small task to develop a project's vision. Sharing a broad, inspiring vision that is hammered out by the core participants, and which is refined as new people and organizations join the project, is the foundation for building ongoing trust and resource commitments. Both HathiTrust and the DPLA see themselves as gateways to the scholarly and cultural record of humanity; NISO's website says that its vision is "a world where all benefit from unfettered exchange of information"; and the Library Publishing Coalition wants to create a publishing landscape that is open, inclusive, and sustainable. Those organizations took time to fully understand and shape an inspiring future.

Clarifying your project's aspirational vision is probably going to be one of the first decisions made by the pre-planning group in conjunction with your governance structure. Starting with aspirational themes helps set the tone early. It says that in this project everyone has a voice, and through compromise, your vision will get as close to a win-win situation as possible. If you have a clear sense of your purpose and your potential to impact the world around you, you'll be surprised by what difficulties can be endured or even overcome.

Participation agreements. As the project progress, good intentions between partners will not be enough. Hammering out an agreement can reveal agendas, including hidden agendas, that help you identify the politics of the situation you're operating in. This is the step where you define mutual expectations, clarify roles and responsibilities, identify accountability measures, and choose conflict resolution processes. You need a mutually binding agreement to ensure that each partner will fulfill its obligations to the cooperative, or which at least makes it more likely that the partners will fulfill their obligations. This agreement should be open to modification as circumstances change in your project development.

Formalize support. Make sure that your authorizing documents are clear and widely distributed. A clear statement of what constitutes success is needed. Make sure the lines of communication are wide open and information goes two ways, between participants and the entity with final authority.

Delegate some tasks and responsibilities. I learned the lesson early on that in any large project, there will be tasks that you won't like or that don't fit closely to your skill set. I acknowledge I am not strong on the legalese that makes up the heart of many cooperative agreements or bylaws. Others may dislike constantly communicating the same message, or navigating with disruptive personalities, two tasks with which I'm comfortable. You should bear in mind that every project manager has different strengths and weaknesses. You will be working with a core group of people on a large-scale initiative, and there are going to be tasks that you should delegate rather than attempt to plow through on your own. Lean into your strengths. You're going to have a million details to manage, so save your energy for where you can be most effective. Delegating tasks that are your personal energy-drainers can help you through difficult times.

Look for an early success. Look for small, easy, and early successes. Several prominent researchers on collaboration, such as Whitney Johnson and Amy Edmondson, have identified trust as crucial to successful partnerships. By starting with a mini-project, you can create a win-win situation that will help foster trust while keeping costs low for participants. An early, small project gives you a chance to ask for ideas, identify the participants' previous experience, seek advice, and observe your potential partners. You'll quickly discover whom you can trust, whom you need to treat with caution, and how well your working groups function together.

Consensus decision-making. You're going to be working with a core group of people, and that group may morph from a pre-planning team into your steering committee (or leadership team). With that group, you want to start small and build consensus and agreement slowly. Plan how you introduce working norms to the group in order to allow people to get to know each other and find a place where they can find consensus. Consensus decisions are ones that everyone in the group can support, though not necessarily love. Reaching consensus takes longer than top-down, bureaucratic decision-making, but it comes with the dividend of increased support and commitment to the project. Check out Lawrence Susskind and Jeffrey Cruikshank's book *Breaking Robert's Rules* to learn more about consensus decision-making.

Give credit away. Be generous in giving others credit, while downplaying your own work. In a 2016 study of 64,000 people across 13 countries, John Gerzema found that sharing credit ranked as the most important quality of a leader, followed by collaboration, flexibility, and selflessness. A bit of modest behavior can pay back dividends.

Build on existing relationships. Work to strengthen your existing personal relationships and create new ones. Collaboration works best when there is an element of interpersonal camaraderie within the project. Try to balance out how much everyone is giving and getting during the long haul of the project. Everyone needs to contribute, and everyone needs a win.

Involve a broad base of participants. Go beyond the same contributors to reach broader participation in your project. Participants bring differing interests and points of view which, if properly facilitated, will create better paths forward for your initiative. Embracing a mindset of openness and inclusion will bring in the widest swath of contributors. Those unique participant viewpoints will ring with more energy than if you find yourself working with the same old group of like-minded libraries doing the same work for the same types of institutions. It is not always clear who your contributors should be, but don't accept the same old stale crowd, even if it is prestigious. What different types of libraries, different sizes of libraries, or different nonprofit organizations might be working in the same zone as your project?

Communication. You will be personally evaluated not just by the success of your final product, but also by the frequency, structure, and quality of the project's communication. Not surprisingly, the most common interaction most participants will have with your initiative will be communicated messages. Communication is your visibility to both the personnel of your project and the outside world of interested libraries. Some of your communication vehicles, such as online or in-person meetings, webinars, newsletters, e-mail lists, social media posts, and conference presentations, will be regularly scheduled, while some will occur as situations change or problems pop up.

A communication team can be your best friend during large-scale project implementation. This team can be as informal as one person or a group of four or five people who coordinate sending a message across different mediums. You should form this working group before you think you need it and have them working on strategies to communicate even before you know what you want to say. This group will become pivotal during the public launch of the initiative.

Project manager's communication. It's a truism that you need to communicate, communicate, and then communicate again. Unfortunately, research shows that people only hear when they're ready to hear, so you will need to be repeating the same messages until you want to scream. As a project leader, I found it most effective to be the primary voice of communication early in the project's development and a leader during online meetings and conference presentations. But out-in-front visibility has a shelf life of its own. If you are constantly appearing in someone's e-mail box, over time they lose interest in what you are saying. As the project progresses, have other people on the team become the messengers for non-critical communication. Limit your voice to when a message is critical.

Communication tools. There are many online tools to manage internal communication. Sometimes these tools are also helpful for external communication as well. Over many projects I've used five software communication tools, all with different strengths and weaknesses. Some of the new tools are multi-modal and quite effective, like Slack or Basecamp. Look into communication systems such as Slack, Dropbox, Basecamp, or Google Groups, but also pay attention to what systems are used by the majority of your participating libraries.

Live your values. Sometimes walking-the-talk is what catches people's attention. Look for ways to demonstrate collaborative values. When we started working on a statewide e-books system in Minnesota, we held six webinars, a one-day workshop, and built out a complex committee structure to get as much input from the wider library community as possible. We were doing a collaborative project and we engaged our community from the beginning.

Take one for the team. You're going to have to model a lot of behaviors that may or may not come naturally to you. But there are a few skills you must master, like consensus-building, acknowledging failure, and giving credit. Partnerships are about sharing power and responsibility. You must demonstrate that you, and the most powerful stakeholders among your participants, will compromise. You may even go so far as to accept some painful compromises early on to show that you have the greater good in mind, not just your own organization's good.

Large-scale projects are balancing acts, and it's often a delicate balance. I have found that if I concentrated on our values and goals while listening and giving credit to others, I could survive a lot of the other mistakes. As far back as the 1990s, William Kahn was talking about the importance of being brave enough to engage with others on your team without fear of consequences to one's self-image, status, or career. To be a large-scale project manager, you will have to be the best you can be.

HARD TIMES

Hard times should pull us together and not apart.

—DONALD IANNONE

As stated at the beginning of this chapter, collaboration can be exhausting and trying. Project management is all about doing hard things. Quite a few library writers have discussed the problems with collaboration. In 1999, Bernard Naylor wrote extensively about the causes of failing consortia in Britain. He concluded that libraries need both more imagination and more perseverance. Greg Pronevitz and I published a study in our 2015 book, *Library Consortia,* that highlighted over seventy consortium failures between 2000 and 2010. Many factors contribute to why collaborative efforts fail, including lack of financial resources, inadequate staff training, inadequate staffing resources, an uninspiring vision and weak goals, and ineffectual leadership.

Stephen Abram has said of library cooperation, "I despise puny visions." If the core goal of your project is not inspiring, you will spend a lot of time fighting the bush fires of discontent instead of moving your project forward. In the next chapter, I talk about the importance of the big idea and how people will get swept along in something remarkable. If people are excited about the outcome, they will cut you more slack on day-to-day problems.

By far the most prevalent reason I've heard for collaboration failures is the participants' fear of losing autonomy. Libraries are often funded by local governments or campus administrations that focus on local circumstances, and that can make justifying your collaborative involvement complicated. In my experience, the issue is also tied to the library leadership not wanting to lose control. But the perceived loss of local autonomy can be compensated for by the additional resources gained through the collaboration. There are no perfect solutions to this dilemma. You need solid commitments from the leadership of participating organizations to get through resistance.

As a project leader, you will spend a large amount of time explaining the benefits of your initiative. Not everyone you work with will come to the table with a strong skill set in negotiations, communication, and interpersonal relations. Librarians are predisposed to want to collaborate, but given the complexity and problems inherent in cooperative efforts, you need to pay attention to the skills and knowledge level of the participants in your project. You may need to either bring in some training programs or send key people to gain facilitation or other skills. I'd recommend building in a training budget just for these circumstances.

Lately, a lot has been written about collaboration overload. The *Harvard Business Review* dedicated a 2016 issue to the topic. Given the typical academic library's involvement in 15–25 cooperative projects, burnout is not just possible, but probable. If enough participants are experiencing collaboration fatigue, it can threaten your project. Time spent in endless meetings is particularly a source of concern from library staff. You need to make sure your meetings are well-run and productive. There are hurdles to be faced in a collaborative project, but as Michael Ridley has said, we collaborate out of self-interest.

THE COLLABORATION EQUATION

A clear purpose will unite you as you move forward, values will guide your behavior, and goals will focus your energy.

—KENNETH H. BLANCHARD

As the preceding sections detailed, collaborative efforts come with both pluses and minuses. And as Michael Ridley reminds us, collaboration must be about the organization's self-interest, or else the willingness to contribute the needed resources will not happen. One way to determine whether the collaboration is worthwhile is to use the collaboration equation:

Total the perceived gains in efficiency, services, and resources
+ Add that to the perceived cost of not making the improvement
– Subtract out the loss of productivity that comes with any
      collaborative project
= The remainder is the value of your collaborative project.

Librarians are rightly cautious about committing to a new cooperative endeavor. It will be worth your while to have the answers to some questions from participants before they are asked:

- Can you clearly and succinctly state the initiative's vision?
- What are the goals to achieve the vision?
- What staff expertise is available on your teams? Or what expertise or skills do you need to gain?
- How will shared decision-making work?
- Who has the final authority to make decisions and at what levels? (Note: a decision authority chart can be worth making.)
- Are your planning and resource commitments fair and equitable?
- Do you have problem resolution strategies predetermined?
- How will you measure your progress?
- How will you evaluate and assess the initiative's outcomes?
- How will you know you succeeded?

That collaboration often requires substantial commitments of time, resources, and staffing should not be underestimated. The commitment to launch into a collaborative process is a commitment to providing extensive resources over time. Collaboration requires an intense and continuous focus on purpose and investment. The literature suggests that those who clearly define the "why" and "how" of collaboration are more likely to succeed.

VALUES-BASED COLLABORATION

Sustaining the culture of collaboration requires vigilance and maintenance.

—MICHAEL RIDLEY

As Lorcan Dempsey has said, as libraries are forced to meet new institutional requirements and patron needs and expectations, the pull towards the collaborative imperative is strong. It makes sense to do things together at the right scale in order to stretch resources, gain experience, and improve customer services.

You should remember that collaboration is a principle as well as a set of necessary actions to be taken during a large-scale initiative. Your project will move forward because a diverse set of people are willing to have a civil dialogue and find compromises. People want to connect, and many are hungry for connection. Remember that collaboration is also about something higher than just achieving your goals, it is a values-based system of action.

Values-based collaboration means:

- Everyone has a voice that will be heard.
- Different ideas will be tolerated and explored.
- Actions will be as transparent as possible.
- Experts' knowledge is valued, but other voices are also heard.
- Leaders work toward the full participation of all participants.

In the end, always remember that you are working to improve library services for our libraries and their patrons.

REFERENCES

Cross, Rob, Reb Rebele, and Adam Grant. "Collaborative Overload." *Harvard Business Review* 94 (2016): 74–79.

Edmondson, Amy. *The Fearless Organization: Creating Psychological Safety in the Workplace for Learning, Innovation, and Growth.* Hoboken, NJ: John Wiley & Sons, 2019.

Gartenberg, Claudine, Andrea Prat, and George Serafeim. "Corporate Purpose and Financial Performance." *Organization Science* 30 (2019): 1–18.

Gerzema, John. "Tomorrow's Leaders Will Be Flexible, Selfless, and Ready to Collaborate." *FastCompany.Com* (blog), May 16, 2013.

Horton, Valerie. "Going 'All-in' for Deep Collaboration." *Collaborative Librarianship* 5 (2013): 65.

Horton, Valerie, and Greg Pronevitz. *Library Consortia: Models for Collaboration and Sustainability*. Chicago: American Library Association, 2015.

Johnson, Whitney. "Collaboration Is Risky. Now, Get on with It." *Harvard Business Review* (blog) (June 7, 2011): 2–4.

Laufer, Alexander, Terry Little, Jeffrey Russell, and Bruce Maas. *Becoming a Project Leader: Blending Planning, Agility, Resilience, and Collaboration to Deliver Successful Projects*. Cham, Switz.: Springer International, 2017.

Lawrence, Gary S. "Radical Change by Traditional Means: Deep Resource Sharing by the University of California Libraries." *Serials* 17 (2004): 119–25.

Machovec, George. "What Library Collaboration Means to Me: Perspectives from an Academic Consortium Director." *Collaborative Librarianship* 11 (2019): 140–43.

Melling, Maxine, and Margaret Weaver. *Collaboration in Libraries and Learning Environments*. London: Facet, 2012.

Montiel-Overall, Patricia. "Toward a Theory of Collaboration for Teachers and Librarians." *School Library Media Research* 8 (January 2005): 1.

Naylor, Bernard. "CURL – Resource Management." *The New Review of Academic Librarianship* 5 (January 1999): 149–57.

Needham, George. "Bottling the Collaboration Thing." *Collaborative Librarianship* 7 (2015): 2.

Ohio State University Libraries. "Definition of Collaboration." Ohio State University Libraries Collaboration Task Force, 2008.

Pisano, Gary P., and Roberto Verganti. "Which Kind of Collaboration Is Right for You?" *Harvard Business Review* 86 (2008): 78–86.

Ridley, Michael. "Culture, Values, and Change: Observations from Three Consortia in Canada." In *Collaboration in Libraries and Learning Environments*. London: Facet, 2012.

Susskind, Lawrence E., and Jeffrey L. Cruikshank. *Breaking Robert's Rules: The New Way to Run Your Meeting, Build Consensus, and Get Results*. New York: Oxford University Press, 2006.

Wheeler, Brad, and James L. Hilton. "The Marketecture of Community." *EDUCAUSE Review* 47 (2012): 66–82.

FIVE

BIG, HAIRY, AUDACIOUS GOALS (BHAG)

RIDING A BHAG

Embrace your responsibility to dream big.

—KEVIN MICHEL

Libraries Transform is a long-standing ALA initiative. What goal is bigger than transforming someone's life? There are times in a library career when going all-in is the way to go. There are times when you want to make a big impact. There is that weird and wonderful place when you are ready to put it all on the line. You want to shake people out of their complacency and have them say, hey, the library did that, wow! If you honestly believe that libraries can transform lives and communities, then grab a big, hairy, audacious goal, or BHAG (pronounced *bee-hag*) and hang on.

The term BHAG was coined by Jim Collins and Jerry Porras in their book *Built to Last*. They described a BHAG as engaging people by reaching out and grabbing them at the gut level. This is the kind of engagement that builds a tangible, energized, and highly focused commitment to a library initiative. People get the BHAG concept and are moved by the profound implications of success. A BHAG, according to Collins, is not a traditional goal. Instead, it

- Is clear and compelling
- Requires little or no explanation

- Pushes people out of their comfort zone
- Requires a heroic effort but can be accomplished
- Is exciting and stimulating

Some librarians instinctively swing for the fences. In the face of a potentially devastating ballot initiative that would have eliminated all statewide support for libraries in Colorado in 2010, the state's librarians, under the leadership of Jamie LaRue, grabbed a BHAG and ran with it. We launched a statewide public relations campaign that recruited community leaders (not librarians) to present a carefully crafted script on how libraries transform lives to civic groups across the state. The project reached over 3,000 people and resulted in a solid defeat for the ballot initiative. Another stretch goal comes from the Iowa City Public Library. They set a goal of having every child in their community becoming a reader and owning a library card. A few years ago, the Public Library Association (PLA) proclaimed its BHAG was to make everyone understand that the public library was the most valued asset in their community.

The PLA's goal created a bit of controversy at the time, but according to Collins, the issue isn't whether you have the perfect goal. The issue is whether the goal you're working toward is clear, compelling, and likely to stimulate people to action. Does your goal create a desire for people to join with you, to be along for the ride, wild or not? Collins emphasizes that it is critical to make your goal fit with the core ideology and values of your organization. No matter what you think of the PLA's choice of a goal, having the public library seen as an asset in every community fits perfectly with our profession's core beliefs.

Read almost any library's strategic plan and you'll find that most people would agree that the listed goals are nice. But "nice" has never inspired anyone. These libraries don't realize that it can be far easier to get buy-in for a big goal that builds enthusiasm. Not all libraries need to have BHAGs. But as Collins says, if you want to get other people to feel that they belong to something special and unique, then grab a big, hairy, and audacious goal!

The rest of this chapter will look at how to work through the ideation process and develop your ambitious goals for a large-scale library project that pushes the boundary of the ho-hum everyday world. For this chapter, suspend your doubt and disbelief and concentrate on the big vision. Dare to inspire!

IDEATION MYTHOLOGY

Far better to dare mighty things, to win glorious triumphs.

—THEODORE ROOSEVELT

Close your eyes and envision Thomas Edison seated in his laboratory, tinkering with one of the 1,093 inventions he patented and shouting *eureka* as the lightbulb turns on. The story of a brilliant inventor struggling alone in his laboratory is embedded deep in the American psyche. Another classic example is Albert Einstein working all by himself on his revolutionary theories. However, a 2015 *Nature* article, "Einstein Was No Lone Genius," found that his landmark relativity theory happened in consultation with a dozen people and some of them, like Marcel Grossmann and Michele Besso, were crucial to his success.

Steven Johnson, in his excellent TED Talk "Where Good Ideas Come From," researched the genesis for innovative ideas. His tagline is that chance favors the connected mind. Johnson's talk highlights the errors associated with the solitary genius myth. He looked for patterns that exist across all types of creative work. He found that great ideas are not single things; they are cobbled together from complex networks that, like a neural network, fire all over the place. He argues that innovation is chaotic and needs numerous ideas colliding and connecting from disparate groups of people in order to work.

Like Steven Johnson, Bill Gates often says that great ideas do not appear in isolation. In public forums, Gates argues that creativity is an emergent property that bubbles up when communities of people attempt to solve problems. He argues that the challenge for today's generation is not finding the new idea, but instead creating organizational structures and cultures that can manage to implement the new idea. The goal of a leader should be to provide the infrastructure and the structural underpinnings needed to reinforce messy collaborations and build on successful ideas.

DISRUPTIVE INNOVATION

Most every innovation—disruptive or not—begins life as a small-scale experiment.

—CLAYTON M. CHRISTENSEN

Clayton Christensen introduced the concept of "disruptive innovation" in his landmark book *The Innovator's Dilemma* in 1997. Work on the theory has continued by researchers at the Harvard Business School. According to Christensen, disruptive innovation threatens and destroys an existing product or service by creating new or value-added products or services. In the past few decades, old products and services have crumbled under the impact of new ideas or technologies at an alarming speed. The classic example is the Blockbuster chain, which had over 4,500 video rental stores in 1990. By 2014, all the stores had closed due to the greater convenience and lower prices offered by DVD mail-order outlets like Netflix.

The theory of disruptive innovation states that established businesses (think libraries here) don't pursue innovative solutions because their dominance in the existing marketplace leads them to reject breakthrough innovations—or "disruptive technologies"—that would threaten or disrupt their own hold on the marketplace. From a library perspective, the concept would be: why should we provide kabuki shows when puppet shows are our bread and butter. That kind of thinking works well until kabuki unexpectedly become the next big thing for preschoolers. One of the features of disruptive technologies is that once the new thing has taken off, it often achieves a much faster takeoff and a higher degree of impact than the established product or service.

In the 1990s, as an academic director, I didn't question our bibliographic instruction program since we had a captive market of freshmen taking English 101 classes. Of course, times changed, and the faculty voted with their feet by choosing to stop offering such instruction during their class time. Few parts of librarianship have changed as much as library instruction has over the past twenty years. As users' information-seeking behaviors rapidly changed, so has the delivery of instruction. The market drives demand, and library leaders can't assume the status quo will remain the same forever.

Christensen found that most organizations are aware of up-and-coming disruptive innovations, but the realities of their current business model don't incentivize them to pursue novel projects. Typically, new products and services are not profitable or popular enough at their launch, they often don't have the full feature set compared to established products and services, and they can take resources away from activities that are currently popular. Consequently, it takes some time for the new disruptive product or service to dominate the marketplace.

Disruptive innovation theory has much to teach us about the need to reinvent library services. We need to prepare for the next big disruption coming at libraries. We'll continue to look at the lessons from Christensen as we discuss how to launch your ideation stage.

HUNTING THE ELUSIVE BHAG

The world needs dreamers, and the world needs doers. But above all what the world needs most are dreamers that do.

—SARAH BAN BREATHNACH

In many ways, the most enjoyable part of working on a large-scale library project is the ideation stage. Here is where you let your imagination run wild and talk to people who don't ordinarily come into your sphere. This is the place where you don't have to worry about limited resources or political infighting.

It's not uncommon for project leaders to abbreviate this stage—to their detriment. Decision-makers may already have a locked-in idea, or they've grabbed the first interesting concept without exploring other options. If you're going to launch a large-scale initiative, you want to make sure you're doing the right project in the right way. This stage might take months: it is okay to ponder and ask different questions, solicit unique perspectives, and stay open to unexpected insights that might reshape your plans.

We know from research by Steven Johnson that it is often the unexpected confluence of ideas that brings about true inspiration. Take the time now to stray outside your normal information channels and seek insight from unexpected sources. Have you talked to people at the ALA's Center for the Future of Libraries? Have you taken the time to refine your idea in the incubator of other people's opinions?

Other questions to ask include:

- Have you asked your local library community what they find novel or exciting?
- Aside from not having enough money, what are local librarians unhappy about?
- What do front-line library staff think is not serving their patrons well?
- Does someone have a project or hobby that grabs your attention?

- Is there some need in the community that is not being met? What services are online booksellers or for-profit academic institutions offering?
- Finally, is there some opportunity no one considered that could revolutionize the work done in your library?

Now is the time to ask these questions and explore the answers to them.

It is not uncommon at the initial stages for project concepts to undergo numerous revisions, sometimes to the point that the original idea is barely recognizable. If you do the exploration work now, you'll solicit the opinions and ideas you need to ensure there is less chance that revisions will come later. Take your time and explore your BHAG.

INFORMAL IDEATION

Ideation is not a synonym for innovation.

—THEODORE LEVITT

Don't dismiss the importance of informal information-gathering. There is freedom at this stage of the project to savor. Informal information-gathering can be particularly effective in the early stage of ideation. I developed the habit of staying in informal information-gathering mode during my career working in library consortia. Before most meetings, I would ask my colleagues from other institutions what was taking up their time. I'd also ask what they had seen or heard that excited them, and I loved their answers because they varied widely but were always amusing. What librarians spend time on is what is important to them and their organization, whether it is solving local problems or developing an exciting new service.

One of the most effective informal techniques I tried involved catching individuals at conferences and asking for a five-minute, one-on-one, private conversation. I intentionally sought out both library leaders and up-and-coming librarians, who often had different and more interesting concerns. I tried to talk to library staff from different library types, sizes, and geographical locations as well. During these informal chats, I would ask the same questions listed above, with a particular focus on anything that happened at the conference that caught their interest. During these informal chats, I would try hard *not* to insert my own point of view. Immediately after the conversations, I would take notes that I later compiled and shared with my management team. My key takeaway from these discussions was that coffee is a great lubricant for gathering information from librarians.

Many informal techniques can be effective in finding or developing your big idea. When you talk to colleagues, tell them you're looking for a big idea to work on in the profession and see how they respond. Their response may help you find your core steering group. The one important thing to keep in mind when using informal communication channels is to not just talk to the people you always talk to. You will need to reach out to the second tier of your acquaintances or to people in the profession you don't know. The good news is that if you ask people about their opinions and insights, most will be glad to share.

FORMAL IDEATION

Where do new ideas come from? The answer is simple: differences.

—NICHOLAS NEGROPONTE

There are several formal tools to help you create or refine your big idea. Many of them are old standbys like brainstorming, but there are new twists on old techniques that can help you seek the input you need to develop or refine your BHAG.

Surveys

Surveys show that surveys never lie.

—NATALIE ANGIER

Conducting surveys has only a limited value for the ideation process. You can gain information about what people are worried about, but I found in survey after survey that the answer would always be lack of funding, local politics, or poor statistics. Remember Henry Ford's famous quote: "If I had asked people what they wanted; they would have said faster horses." This sentiment is true at the ideation stage. Survey respondents seldom think about big-picture changes that could improve the library profession.

Don't spend your valuable time generating high-quality survey tools when that time could be better spent interacting with people and finding ways to encourage them into big-picture thinking. You should aim to follow

Steven Johnson's advice and find ways to collide the thought and opinions of a host of people from different walks of life. Your informal conversations will give you the insight that a survey never could. So leave the survey behind and choose another option.

Brainstorming

The best idea is to have a lot of ideas.

—BARRY KUDROWITZ

Don't skip over this section, because brainstorming is better than you think! Brainstorming has been around for decades for a reason. It's inexpensive, relatively easy to do, and it usually works. The term *brainstorming* was popularized in a 1942 book by Alex Osborn entitled *How to Think Up*. Brainstorming typically involves an unstructured group offering suggestions and alternate options to solve a problem. A leader keeps the conversation on track, records suggestions, encourages everyone to talk, and wraps up the session. Brainstorming sessions can be used as a tool for identifying and synthesizing offered suggestions. The open-discussion nature of brainstorming makes it a poor choice for group decision-making, however. A large part of brainstorming's bad reputation comes from people trying to turn it into a decision-making tool. Brainstorming works best at the early stage of idea generation.

Alex Osborn argues that to be efficient, those who facilitate brainstorming sessions need to keep two principles in mind. First, defer judgment on the things discussed during the session. By withholding criticism of an expressed idea, you can increase the attendees' willingness to share their suggestions. The second principle is to go for quantity of ideas and suggestions. Osborn believes that quantity breeds quality. The more ideas produced, the better the odds that an unexpected and novel solution will be found. Brainstorming leaders should encourage freewheeling and uninhibited thinking and even playful, but safe, banter.

Some experts argue that brainstorming is a poor setting for introverts, so they now recommend sharing the questions in advance to give people time to mull over the topic, or allotting a few minutes in the beginning for people to think about the questions before you start the discussion. A technique that worked well for me was to give the group the questions and let them take notes about their answers for the first five minutes of the session. The act of note-taking can help some people make better connections and come up with more original suggestions.

One study published in the *Harvard Business Review* by Marion Poetz found that bringing in people who work in very different occupations added power and innovation to group creativity. When groups looked at designing safety equipment for speed ice skaters, the most original ideas did not come from other in-line skaters but from roofers, who also dealt with many safety equipment concerns. Poetz found that the greater the distance between the two analogous fields, the greater the novelty of their solutions. You should expand the normal boundaries where librarians typically function if you want to gain new ideas and new perspectives. This is a BHAG exercise, so go big in your invitations. See what happens. The next great idea may come from the coffee shop owner or the assistant tennis coach.

Brainwriting or Round-Robin Brainstorming

Brainwriting is brainstorming on steroids.

—LITEMIND.COM

Brainwriting or round-robin brainstorming was developed in Germany in the late 1960s by Bernd Rohrbach. The process is designed to encourage group safety by reducing the impact of strong personalities who can dominate a session. In brainwriting, you have everyone write an idea on a large index card, called an idea card. The process is done in silence and criticism is not allowed. Pass the idea card to the next person in the circle and the new person expands or builds upon the idea on the card. Continue swapping the card in the circle until everyone has commented on all the idea cards.

When you've completed the circle, the person who originated the index card will have various suggestions. That card originator can then summarize the results of the round-robin. The facilitator should be recording the main ideas on flip charts while eliminating duplicates. Like brainstorming, brainwriting is for idea generation, but is not a good tool for decision-making.

Brainwriting is a great starting point for an ideation session and can serve as a tool for further idea refinement as a meeting goes on. I have been a participant in several brainwriting sessions, and found that people generally felt they had a voice in the process. In my opinion, the method worked best with groups of people who don't know each other as an icebreaker introductory exercise. With groups that know each other very well, simple brainstorming is faster and probably more efficient.

Focus Groups

The most powerful people on earth are focus groups.

—WILLIAM J. CLINTON

Focus groups, like brainstorming, are ubiquitous in libraries and have been around since their development in the 1940s at Columbia University as a market research tool. These small gatherings allow participants to interactively discuss a specific issue or topic. Participants are asked about their perceptions, beliefs, opinions, and attitudes about a topic. Interactions within the group are encouraged. These groups are often used in libraries for evaluation purposes. State libraries also tend to rely on focus groups to evaluate the impact of federal grants.

Participants are asked open-ended questions and are lightly guided by the moderator. The questions tend to have a more controversial or provocative nature and try to get to the participants' true thoughts and preferences. The size of the focus group varies based on its purpose, but typically falls between 6 and 12 people. Transcripts and records are frequently taken. The questions start easy and get more specific and pointed as time progresses. A skilled moderator is more crucial here than with brainstorming, and the leader needs to have some training and have no stake in the outcome. There are techniques for phone or internet focus groups, but face-to-face sessions remain the most common method. An interesting variant on online focus groups is a trend toward a series of one-on-one conversations with a moderator rather than group discussions.

Nominal Group Technique

The nominal group technique is commonly used when opinions about a potential solution are sought. In this ideation process, 25–50 people are divided into smaller groups of 5–6 people each. Each group is given a problem and is required to compose a list of ideas to solve it. Once each group has developed its list of solutions (often using simple brainstorming), the group is asked to select the best idea from their list; they flesh that idea out and present the selected idea back to the larger group on a marker board or flip chart.

After this stage, the small groups move from flip chart to flip chart and refine or expand upon the concept. After all the groups have gone around, then other techniques like straw polls are used to rank or rate the listed solutions. Research has found that using the more focused approach of the nominal group technique generally produces higher-quality alternatives than simple brainstorming.

Storyboarding

In this ideation process, everyone is given lots of mid-sized sticky notepads. A question is posed to the group, and as fast as possible participants are asked to put their ideas on the sticky notes in a few words or short sentences or even by drawing. They put the first sticky note on the table and quickly add another idea to the table. Speed is important here. After all the ideas are generated, the group starts clustering the ideas in clumps. For instance, if the question was: how do we improve attendance at the children's story hour, you would cluster sticky notes that say more Punch and Judy shows, more kabuki theater, or more cookies into separate groups.

The clusters should be added to wall-mounted flip charts so people can see how ideas interact or connect. The act of putting the sticky notes on the board and arranging the notes within the new clusters reveals deeper relationships between the different ideas. For more depth, you can have people select a sticky note cluster and further develop the ideas. A winnowing process will let you eliminate extraneous ideas and organize the remaining ideas in a series that shows the importance of each idea.

The storyboarding technique can also be valuable when you have a complex idea and want to isolate a component. As an example, say your project is writing a new book. You could put up large flip chart pages with the headings Chapter 1, Chapter 2, and so on written on each poster. You can then use sticky notes to add content to each chapter and see the book content laid out in a visual presentation. There are quite a few online storyboarding programs as well.

Mind Mapping

Mind mapping allows you to organize your idea in a series of visual relationships. It starts with the big idea and lets you break that idea down into smaller parts. Write down your question or problem at the center of a large whiteboard. Draw concentric circles around that idea. In the first circle out, expand on the idea with terms or data that best describe what you want to see happen. In the next concentric circle out, start adding ways of solving the problem. Keep expanding or building out secondary circles until you have broken down the problem into manageable pieces.

Using colors can help with mind maps, and you don't have to use concentric circles. You can draw lines with bubbles at the end or have rays coming off like branches on a tree. The visualization aspect is key, not the method of organizing your map. Often natural associations seem to mysteriously appear when presented visually. Online mind-mapping tools are becoming popular and there are lots of them online, both free and at substantial prices.

The Delphi Technique

The Delphi technique is used when group members are geographically separated. Each group member is asked to provide ideas in response to a specific question. Their input can be by e-mail, fax, online discussion, or by using group decision-making software such as Google Survey, Qualtrics, Delphi2, Mesydel, or Welphi. All the solutions are shared with the group and with a deadline, and then the participants must rate and rank the ideas and explain their reasoning. The lower-ranked solutions drop off after each round. Many rounds of individual ranking can take place until the best idea or solution is left. The Delphi technique is an ideation tool and can serve as a decision-making tool as well.

FROM IDEATION TO ACTION

New ideas pass through three periods: 1) It can't be done.
2) It probably can be done, but it's not worth doing. 3) I knew it was a good idea all along!

—ARTHUR C. CLARKE

After you've gone through the ideation process, you will have either found an idea or refined your kernel of an idea into a deeper concept. The process of ideation is collaborative, so you will be laying the foundations for future relationships that will become crucial to your project's success. This is the stage to take a minute to circle back to Clayton Christensen's work. Is your idea

- An improvement to an existing library product or service?
- A new product or service that is not currently offered through libraries?

As we move out of the initiation stage of project development into the planning stage, you need to have a firm understanding of the answers to these two questions. How you design your plan, how you communicate about it, and how you think about your work will be fundamentally impacted by whether you are working on a new product or whether you are improving an existing product or service. Having a firm handle on what realm you're working in will shape how your project develops from this stage forward. It will impact (1) who you invite to work with you on the project, (2) how you will obtain resources, and (3) how you will market the newly launched product or improved service to your patrons.

The next two chapters deal with planning. This is where you start fleshing out your idea with details, solidifying your resources and partners, and setting up the infrastructure to do a large-scale library initiative.

REFERENCES

Christensen, Clayton M. *The Innovator's Dilemma: The Revolutionary Book That Will Change the Way You Do Business.* New York: Harper Business, 2011.

Collins, James C., and Jerry I. Porras. *Built to Last: Successful Habits of Visionary Companies.* New York: HarperBusiness Essentials, 2002.

Janssen, Michel, and Jürgen Renn. "Einstein Was No Lone Genius." *Nature* 527 (2015): 298–300.

Johnson, Mark W., Clayton M. Christensen, and Henning Kagermann. "Reinventing Your Business Model." *Harvard Business Review* 86 (December 1, 2008): 50.

Johnson, Steven. *Where Good Ideas Come from: The Natural History of Innovation.* New York: Riverhead Books, 2011.

Kim, Jim Yong. "What I Learned from Bill Gates." *The Washington Post* (Washington, D.C), 2014-05-19.

Osborn, Alex Faickney. *How to Think Up.* New York: McGraw-Hill, 1942.

Poetz, Marion, Franke, Nikolaus, and Martin Schreier. "Sometimes the best ideas come from outside your industry." *HBR Blog* (November 21, 2014).

SIX

SETTING THE STAGE

CREATING GOOD FORTUNE

Good fortune is what happens when opportunity meets with planning.

—THOMAS EDISON

The initiation stage of your project is over. You are now moving into stage two, the *planning* stage. Your big idea has been expanded and refined. You followed an inclusive process to get to planning, and you've already worked with your initial stakeholders and participants. Now is the time to start setting up the structures that will serve as the foundation for your project. Planning is not a small operation, and almost everyone who writes about project management cautions readers not to skimp on or rush through this stage. There are a lot of people who want to jump in and start working on the project right away, but remember, as Winston Churchill said, "planning is essential."

SCOPING IT OUT

The preliminary project scope statement specifies what should be the goals and objectives of the project and what needs to be accomplished.

—SIRAJ QURESHI

Throughout this book we have been discussing scope, an important topic that frames your entire project. Scope is important enough to be thought of as having three components:

1. Developing scope
2. Managing scope
3. Assessing scope

Defining your project's scope should be one of the first tasks you tackle. You have already developed your central idea, and now it is time to turn that into a pre-scope statement, or a preliminary scope statement if you prefer. This statement will serve as the framework for the entire planning document that we discuss in the next chapter.

A pre-scope statement helps you further refine the realities of implementing your idea, deepens buy-in, and sets the tone for the project. This pre-scope work should be addressed as part of an early statement of project work that will be refined as more information is gathered during planning. This preliminary statement frames your objectives, project deliverables, and an early estimate of resources needed. You want a clear definition here of what you hope to achieve with this project. The preliminary scope document will be one of the first outputs from your project, so make it professional.

The pre-scope statement can serve as the skeleton for the full planning document you will produce after you've had time to fully research all your options. It is important at this stage to take the time to think out the scope of the project, and to discuss possibilities with stakeholders, participants, and governing authorities. The preliminary scope document typically includes these sections:

- *Description and Purpose*: Describe the project and what it will accomplish. This includes an early consideration of how the project's outcomes will impact system users.
- *Early Objectives*: It may be too early to get specific, measurable, achievable, realistic, and time-based (or SMART) objectives written. But start aiming for SMART statements that you will continue to enhance throughout the planning process.

- *Resources*: This is a preliminary assessment of the resources needed to develop the new system or service. These resources include possible vendors and financial, physical, and human capital needs.
- *Constraints and Risks*: This section assesses the known limits on your resources, and what potential situations could derail or increase the project's costs. It is best to get possible negatives out in public view as early as possible; hiding negatives never pays off in the long run.
- *Preliminary Deliverables, Timelines, and Milestones*: This is your best estimate of the time when you will be able to produce deliverables and the critical steps that must happen to achieve your milestones. This is a preliminary assessment, and it is okay to indicate that any date is subject to revision in the full plan.
- *Team Structure*: This is a rudimentary organizational structure for the project, including the leadership team, the working groups, and proposed communication channels.

Many of these steps are launch pads for further discussion. You should expect topics like the resources needed and the team structure to be heavily modified by stakeholders and potential partners. You're going to want to use terms like "preliminary," "draft," and "for further discussion" liberally in the document to signal that you are starting the discussion, not locking in decisions before wider participation has been sought. The project design will change as planning goes on, but with this document, you establish the parameters of the initial discussion. That's a powerful place for you to get your ideas out early in the process. Make use of this opportunity!

PLANNING DOWN TO THE BONES

Project management can be defined as a way of developing structure in a complex project.

—RORY BURKE

As your preliminary scope document is being publicly discussed, you are probably starting work on the actual planning document you will need to get final approval for the project. The whole point of establishing a project's organizational structure is to lay a foundation to allow you to move forward. The second and equally important point of establishing structure is to open communication channels that will become critical as the project matures. Other items considered part of project structures include leadership, team organization, reporting relationships, and proposed communication channels.

A small-scale library project may have a lead and a support person, and potentially technical support. Large-scale library projects can have a massive infrastructure. The HathiTrust Digital Library, for example, has 12 staffers, 14 members on the governance committee, 5 executive committee members, 13 people on the program steering committee, and around 11 task forces or subcommittees, though these numbers vary. Obviously, few projects are as large or as successful as HathiTrust, but don't underestimate the library community's desire for complexity.

You'll be spending a lot of time in discussions about the project's structure, and everyone will have opinions. Librarians take structure seriously and for good reason. When I'm looking at a new library service I've never heard of before, I look first for the mission and participants, and then at the organizational structure. Structure gives experienced librarians a lot of information about the project. Which libraries, individuals, and other organizations are participating? How big is this project? Is it collaborative or bureaucratic? The structure tells the observer whether there are thought-leaders involved and if the project has credibility. It reveals political astuteness or naivete, as well as the depth of expertise and resources available.

I recommend that you spend considerable time looking at the organizational structure of similar projects. A new digital library will have a different structure than a project for bringing up a new, open-source catalog. When you propose your organizational structure, be sure to state that this is the initial design, with more refinements to come. Give yourself space to change as the project matures. This will be a good time to find a senior mentor or advisor with an excellent reputation to work with you before you present the preliminary proposal to decision-makers. Someone who has been involved in large-scale library initiatives for years might see pitfalls that you could easily miss.

James P. Lewis argues that most projects don't have problems with tools, but with people. The structure you set up to manage people will either aid you or impede you. If you don't have a lot of experience with managing people and politics, this is another time to turn to mentors and advisors.

INNOVATORS, EARLY ADOPTERS, AND OTHER PIPE DREAMS

Just because someone doesn't jump on board immediately, doesn't mean they won't jump on board eventually.

—DAVID ARRINGTON

Your planning document will need to include a section on the potential participants in your project. There is theoretical work that can help you structure your plan to appeal to prospective adopters. If you craft your plan correctly, the document can serve not just to reassure funders and decision-makers that your project is viable, but can also serve as a selling point for those considering joining in.

The "diffusion of innovation" theory has become well known since it was created by Everett Rogers in 1962, largely due to the 1990s technology boom. Rogers's book *Diffusion of Innovations* is in its fifth edition. Based on decades of research and spanning many academic disciplines, the theory has continued to be discussed due to the sheer number of projects that have validated its thesis. With the diffusion of innovation theory, Rogers wanted to identify how new ideas and technology spread into a specific community.

Rogers's principal argument is that a new idea spreads primarily through social interactions. His research identified four elements that influence the diffusion of a new concept: (1) the innovation itself, (2) the communication channels used, (3) the length of time involved, and (4) a community or social system where the information can spread. His main finding is that human capital is needed to obtain widespread adoption.

Rogers identified five types of participants in the adoption of a new technology:

- *Innovators* (2.5 percent of the potential population): These participants are defined by a willingness to take risks. This group has high social status, strong financial resources, and are integrated into social networks within the community. Innovators are comfortable with risk and failure.
- *Early Adopters* (13.5 percent): This includes a high proportion of opinion leaders. Like innovators, early adopters have high status and solid financial resources, but are likely to pay attention to political considerations and potential benefits as they make judicious decisions.

- *Early Majority* (34 percent): These participants have above-average social status, adequate resources, and many connections within the social community but are seldom thought-leaders.
- *Late Majority* (34 percent): These participants are somewhat skeptical and cautious, and are likely to have lower-than-average social status in the community and fewer financial assets.
- *Laggards* (16 percent): These participants tend to have low social status, offer no opinion leadership, and are most likely to be averse to change. Laggards focus on maintaining traditions and have few financial resources.

According to Rogers, the essential measure of project success is having reached the critical mass of adopters needed to create a self-sustaining infrastructure. In 2013, the Digital Public Library of America (DPLA) started with six Service Hubs (or innovators): the one I managed, the Minnesota Digital Library, along with digital libraries in Georgia, Kentucky, Massachusetts, South Carolina, and the Mountain West. By 2015, the DPLA had 1,600 early adopters and 10 million digital items in its catalog. By 2020, that number had grown to 5,044 unique contributors and 39 million items in the database. Seven years after its launch, DPLA was moving through early majority adopters into the pool of late majority adopters in a phenomenally successful and fast growth curve.

At the start, you will be working closely with your innovators and probably some early adopters as well. To reach high levels of participation, Rogers argues that you need to use your communication channels with groups that exist in your social system; that is, libraries, funders, and cultural heritage institutions. To know how to reach these different groups, you need to understand the process that organizations go through to decide to join a collaborative. The five stages of the process are:

1. *Knowledge*: Potential adopters become aware of your project but still don't have enough information about it to form an opinion.
2. *Awareness/Persuasion*: Potential adopters become inspired to seek out more information about your project. There is growing chatter about your project among peer groups.
3. *Evaluation*: Action is taken to evaluate your project, seeking to determine whether it will provide a perceived improvement over the current system. Potential participants are weighing the pros and cons of change.

4. *Trial Implementation*: A trial is undertaken next to make sure that the new system is compatible with existing structures, whether it is relatively easy to learn, and whether the new system has other potentials not initially anticipated.

5. *Continuation*: The process ends with the decision to adopt your system and become part of the collaborative.

According to Rogers, the impact of your system will be judged according to numerous factors in a complex decision-making process. Innovators move through those stages at lightning speed, often minimizing some steps, while the late majority adopters sit back and judge every step you take.

Pay attention to those who find unexpected uses for your system. In my experience, some of the most significant growth in projects I have been involved with came from individuals who found a use for our system we didn't initially predict. Those unexpected and serendipitous system uses should dominate your public relations materials. It's the unexpected that tends to catch the attention of those considering adopting your system and can play an oversized role in the impression your project makes on the greater world.

Rogers recommends using high-status individuals within the social group to proselytize your message, but to also use a variety of voices ranging from traditionalists (gatekeepers) to up-and-coming upstarts (thought-leaders) as part of your voice out into the community. Make sure you give those voices credible messages to deliver.

ORGANIZING TIGERS

"Never doubt that a small group of thoughtful, committed citizens can change the world; indeed, it's the only thing that ever has."

—MARGARET MEAD

When working on large-scale library projects, you are going to be working with a lot of people. This section will look at the roles you will need to fill and how to organize your workers, stakeholders, and participants. It helps to think of these groups in different layers moving out from a central core of the project management team. Each group will require its particular communication, interactions, and work requirements. Having a model for grouping people can help simplify how you think and act during the project.

Group Organization Models

Every team must deal with goals, roles, responsibilities, procedures, and relationships.

—JAMES P. LEWIS

Think of your participant structure as being a set of concentric circles: at the center of the ring is you and your staff, and the furthest ring from you is patrons.

1. *Inner ring*: Project manager, support staff, information technology staff
2. *Closest ring*: Project teams, governing body
3. *Next ring*: Stakeholders, partners, advisors
4. *Outreach ring*: Libraries, museums, library groups, cultural heritage organizations
5. *Outer ring*: Patrons, users, other library staff

Use a structure that makes sense to your project; this may not be a document you share, but it can help you see how to prioritize your limited time.

Your stakeholders and supporters may change over the course of a large-scale initiative. You will quickly identify who are your key go-to people, who you need to keep in the information loop, and who you want to keep at arm's length. At a more granular level, it helps to have a model that organizes stakeholders into logical groups, from critical groups to those with some potential.

These groups are not static. You can have a library that is committed to working on your project with major resource commitment, and then a change of leadership disrupts that intention. The alternative is just as likely: an uninterested library suddenly discovers the benefits of your project and comes in with a substantial commitment of time, resources, and people. Keep flexibility in mind as you design your structure and systems.

Project Manager

The primary responsibility of the project manager is to ensure that all work is completed on time, within budget and scope, and at the correct performance level.

—JAMES P. LEWIS

The project manager is the most visible and critical role in any large-scale library initiative. Think of the project manager as the person who makes it all happen, the conductor who keeps a zillion details in mind, and yet has time for a cup of coffee with a team member. Yes, this is our library superhero.

Well over a hundred years ago, Mary Parker Follett coined the saying: "Management is the art of getting things done through people." In libraries, people who have technical, performance, or research competence are crucial to our success, and you need those people on your teams. In contrast, technical skills are helpful but not required for a project manager. The project manager needs to have outstanding people skills, strong organization abilities, solid emotional intelligence, and a mastery of budget magic. In the end, the manager will be judged not just on the project's overall success, but also on their people, communication, and budgetary skills. This reality often surprises newbies who focus on technical competence, but I've seen it play out time and again in libraries.

Focusing on people is key to the project manager's success. Marcus Buckingham surveyed employees from more than 80,000 organizations and identified the number one trait of good managers. It is the ability to find the best, most unique features of each person and capitalize on those traits to enhance the overall goals of the organization. Using these skills allows you to plug a person's unique talents and technical skills into tasks that need to be completed. By definition, this means you're going to need a project team that's okay with somewhat fluid assignments. Focusing on each person's strengths has the added value of enhancing accountability and building a stronger sense of team spirit, since each person is contributing at their highest level.

In my experience, the next most important focus a project manager needs to have is a commitment to accountability, respect, and integrity. The project manager must be seen to be walking the walk of ethical honesty, and must routinely look at decisions through the prism of fairness, accountability, and integrity. Accountability means you are making sure your team is performing on time, is making good choices, and is alerting people to problems and successes. The Project Management Institute has a Code of Ethics and Professional Conduct online, as does the American Library Association. Your goal is not to grandstand on this issue, but to apply the routine and careful application of the best principles of librarianship and project management to yourself and your team's actions.

I've said that accountability and ethics are among the most important traits a project manager must demonstrate daily, and I believe that, but there is another important trait—the ability to communicate. Never underestimate the importance of communication that moves both up and down the hierarchy. Marill and Lesher found that as much as 90 percent of a manager's time can be spent on communication.

Communication is complicated by the fact that people only hear what they want to hear when it's on their time or in their interest. This means you must repeat messages over and over again on a variety of communication channels. Also, no matter how much effort you put into communication, be prepared to be criticized. It comes with the territory. Do your best, slough off criticisms that don't help, and use the criticisms that do help to do better. Project managers must always be reaching for their best selves no matter what the provocation.

In the best-case scenarios, the project manager has had training in the skills related to running large-scale operations; however, libraries are filled with staff members who learned on the job as they went along. Most universities and community colleges offer project management training, much of it online. Three primary associations govern project management, the aforementioned Project Management Institute (PMI), the International Project Management Association (IPMA), and Axelos: Global Best Practices. Spend time on their websites or in their classes to learn more from the best. There are also endless project management books; you can start by reading everything written by James P. Lewis.

Project Sponsor

Successful initiation of a new project is always based upon project sponsorship.

—ERIC McCONNELL

On occasion you may hear the term *project sponsor* in academic libraries, and more rarely in public libraries. In project management literature, however, sponsorships occupy a central role. A project sponsor is an intermediary, and hopefully a champion, between the project manager and the sponsoring organization(s). You can think of the project sponsor as an advocate who has a vested interest in benefiting from the results of the project and is committed to supporting the project and persuading others to help. You may have more than one project sponsor, but if you have three or more it can add complexity and alignment difficulties.

This person, typically a senior manager, is the contact between the project manager and the governing authority. The project sponsor should be an ally, helping to support the project manager and the leadership team. The project sponsor coordinates with funders to serve as a sounding board, helps resolve budget issues, works to remove obstacles and conflicts, and signs off on necessary approvals. The sponsor can also be a source of great help to the project manager with issues like scope creep or recalcitrant partners.

Stakeholders

Stakeholder: anyone who has a vested interest in the project.

—JAMES P. LEWIS

Stakeholder is a nebulous term, as illustrated by the quote from James P. Lewis above. The Project Management Institute defines a stakeholder as any organization that is impacted by your project, or more significantly, which perceives itself as being affected by the activities and outcomes of your project. The *Encyclopedia of Management*'s definition of *stakeholders* focuses on the individuals and groups that are affected by the decisions and actions taken. The primary stakeholders are usually your boss, your colleagues, your organization, and your customers.

Your project's sponsoring organization is always considered a stakeholder, and is often the 800-pound gorilla of stakeholders. Many different individuals, groups, and organizations can fall under the definition of a "stakeholder," including project teams and team members, libraries, cultural heritage organizations, charities and granters, government entities, academic administrations, social groups, employees, vendors and suppliers, the media, and the community the library serves. In some cases, your stakeholders volunteer to be in your project rather than being invited to join.

Most planning groups do a brainstorming exercise to determine who the stakeholders are. That's a good idea early in the project. Try to determine who can influence your project in either a negative or positive way, and how much impact they can have. There are questions you should ask such as: What are my stakeholders' priorities? What do they need from this project to be successful? What information do they need from our team? Do they have connections to other granters or political entities that could further the project?

You will probably want to break the stakeholders down into a taxonomy that indicates the crucial groups, as compared to those who are merely interested. Lynda Bourne suggests that key stakeholders change over time, and you should focus on different stakeholders at different times in a project's life cycle. Her model, called "stakeholder circles," provides a useful framework for organizing different types of stakeholders. It can help you make decisions about how to communicate and connect outward to those groups based on their degree of importance to the project.

Project Leadership Team

The all-powerful *steering committee* continued to exercise control.
—ANONYMOUS

Large-scale projects almost always utilize some form of team structure. According to the *Encyclopedia of Management*, a team is a group of people coming together to accomplish a purpose. The *Encylopedia* identifies six types of teams: informal (social), traditional (functional, leadership-appointed), problem-solving (temporary, cross-functional), leadership (steering, advisory), self-directed (no individual status, team authority), and virtual (geographically disparate). The leadership team can go by many names, such as the steering committee, planning team, executive committee, management team, coordinating committee, or just the project team.

The project leadership team may start as a planning committee and morph into an ongoing steering committee that will be with you from the start of the project concept until the sign-off. Typically, the steering committee is composed of librarians with line or staff decision-making authority with regard to some element of the resources you will need. In libraries, it is not uncommon for the heads of communications, information technology, technical services, research support, or outreach services to be included on the committee.

Each leadership team member is often given responsibility for one of the working groups, but they can also be key specialists like communication or human relations experts without committee assignments. The leadership team is the *main* tool available to the project manager to get the job done, and you'll need this team to support you by planning, directing, controlling, and assessing the work that is done. If there is a place where the rubber hits the road, it is with this group of people.

The leadership team will be the group that you share almost all information with, since they'll need to know the most in order to manage the task groups they supervise. In most cases, each leadership team member will have a specific area of focus or work. These areas could be vendor selection, software implementation, policy development, training, networking, finance oversight, public relations, and so on. In close coordination with the project manager, the leadership team will develop documentation and make sure that tasks stay on target.

This group will help develop the originating documents, secure resources, and judge change requests that come in. You'll need this group to help you when scope creep starts, as it may well do. This is the team that will assist you with budgets, milestones, and deliverables and will tell you if you're going off track. If you're lucky, this is the group that will tell you what you need to hear even when you don't want to hear it.

If possible, try to put your political appointees in other positions and keep your leadership team reserved for those who have true expertise, resources, or clout and can move the project forward. Sponsors and stakeholders may want to be in this group, and in the future that may be appropriate, but in the early stage, try to restrict the leadership team to the people who actually oversee and do the work.

Team Members

Teams don't just happen—they must be built!

—JAMES P. LEWIS

Team members are the individuals who perform the ordinary day-to-day work of the project. They are organized into working groups or "teams," each of which is led by a member of the leadership team. Some team members stay throughout the entire project, while others come into the project for a specific task and then leave. Some work full-time, though in my experience most team members work only part-time on library projects. In large-scale initiatives, team members are often drawn from the staff of participating libraries, a consortium, or partner organizations. On large projects the team members can be quite diverse, depending on the nature of the project and the administrative overlords. I have been on project teams that included librarians, potential users, vendors, open-source developers, university staff, city employees, business owners, potential users, and researchers.

Team members will adopt a wide variety of roles, but all contribute to the project objectives in some fashion (if they don't, try to get them off the team), work on specific deliverables, and provide expertise and advice. They also serve the crucial role of helping to spread the word about the project to the wider community.

No one comes to a team with all the knowledge they need, though the closer you can get to experienced people the better. There are several advantages to having a mix of newbies and experienced librarians on your teams. Sometimes a mixture of fresh perspectives with seasoned experience can generate new insights when it's time to make decisions. Try to set aside some funds for training or team-building. I have never seen a team-building exercise that didn't generate a lot of complaining, but I've also seen smart ones that helped gel a team into a cohesive unit. If you're going to do team-building, find an expert and listen to them. A large-scale project is not the time to try a do-it-yourself solution.

You're going to need people with technical skills and library expertise on your project. For instance, the DPLA needed metadata, digital standards, and web-design experts on its teams. Having people with problem-solving or interpersonal skills can be helpful. A thought-leader who is networked into the wider library community can also be a big advantage. There is an unfortunate tendency to focus on technical skills and discount human relationship skills when building a team; this tendency has worked to the detriment of many projects.

You are likely to have individuals you want to recruit for your project. Make sure you check with the potential recruit's supervisor or director before inviting them on. Other times you will be given names to put on the team without having a say in the matter. If possible, play your power cards to get the people you need on your leadership team, and place unwanted others on the working groups with as good a grace as you can muster. Remember, large-scale initiatives are always political. Brian Irwin's research found that projects seldom fail for technical reasons. Their downfall is lack of attention to the political environment, unwillingness to use a flexible style of leadership, and the difficulties of team interpersonal conflicts.

REPORT IT OUT

Being a project manager means creating a ton of project documents.

—ESTHER COHEN

You will want a way to organize and present your preliminary thoughts about your project. Many large libraries and consortia have developed templates to do this. Project management literature is filled with online examples of preliminary planning documents. Below is the outline of the project initiation document we developed at one of my previous jobs. Work closely with your sponsor and advisors to flesh out concepts unique to your project. Creating this document can help shape your thinking as you fill out its various sections.

1. *Background and Purpose*: a brief description of the project, portrays intent
2. *Group Formation*: composition of the teams or working groups
3. *Project Sponsor(s)*: an authority who will advocate for the project
4. *Project Team Members*: consider skills, views, and politics. Sometimes this list may be skills needed, like an HTML expert, or it may be specific people
5. *Group Formation*: the structure of your teams and reporting relationships
6. *Project Manager(s)*: highlight the project manager's expertise
7. *Project Stakeholders*: at this stage, these may be your earliest adopters, or it may be a wider look at who will soon be involved
8. *Project Scope*: what are the boundaries of the project? What will be included or excluded?
9. *Project Outcome*: what will change or improve because of your work, including assessment plans. You may include output measures as well, if appropriate
10. *Decision-Making Authority*: the person who gives the final go-ahead to start the project and end it

11. *Project Timeline*: start and end dates, and key milestones
12. *Communication*: the expectations for reporting to stakeholders, participants, and interested observers
13. *Project Budget*: what resources you will need, obviously an estimate at this early stage
14. *Barriers and Other Issues*: don't ignore problems; lay them out for readers so they know you have plans to mitigate them
15. *Conclusion*: end on a positive note, showing your enthusiasm for the upcoming work

Expect a lot of comments and negotiations on your preliminary plan. The discussions around a preliminary plan are a good time to learn about the political landscape and potential land mines that lay ahead. Once you have gotten a preliminary go-ahead, you move on to the full planning process, which is the topic for the next chapter.

REFERENCES

Bourne, Lynda. *Making Projects Work: Effective Stakeholder and Communication Management*. Boca Raton, FL: CRC, 2015.

Buckingham, Marcus. "What Great Managers Do." *Harvard Business Review* 83 (2005): 70–148.

Encyclopedia of Management. 6th ed. Detroit, MI: Gale, 2009.

Irwin, Brian. "Politics, Leadership, and the Art of Relating to Your Project Team." Paper presented at the PMI Global Congress 2007. Newtown Square, PA: Project Management Institute, 2007.

Lewis, James P. *Fundamentals of Project Management*. 4th ed. New York: American Management Association, 2007.

Marill, Jennifer L, and Lesher, Marcella. "Mile High to Ground Level." *The Serials Librarian* 52 (2007): 317–22.

Rogers, Everett M. *Diffusion of Innovations*. 5th ed. New York: Free Press, 2003.

SEVEN

THE DEVIL IN THE DETAILS

DETAILS, DETAILS, DETAILS

The devil's in the detail and sometimes if you're thinking too big, you can miss the detail.

—BILL BAILEY

The Project Management Institute's PMBOK Guide defines "a project as a temporary activity designed to create a unique product, service, or result." They go on to say that projects have a discrete beginning and an end with a clear result that was established from the start. A project management plan is a path to achieve those results using tools to help schedule tasks, direct tasks, and control resources. We have been working at the 30,000-foot level up until now in the project management process, but now is the time to dive down into the details and start working on specifics. The project plan is your way of capturing those details and sharing information about them with your stakeholders and other interested parties.

A project management plan's core function is to answer questions about scope, time frames, budgets, activities, resources, and responsibilities. Almost any large-scale library initiative will require a formal approach to be used to develop the project plan. Large-scale projects are complex and need the controls and logistical tools that formal project management practices provide. Planning is not a step to take lightly, to rush through, or to do with less than your best work.

GOALS ARE EASY

Common, shared objectives are the obvious core of any collaborative. It is surprising, therefore, that many cooperative ventures lack a clear articulation of exactly what they are.

—MICHAEL RIDLEY

This section's title, "Goals Are Easy," is meant to be a bit tongue-in-cheek. Goals only look easy when they're done right. Before launching into goal-setting, you should start with definitions. Terminology is important to librarians and can be contentious. There are many different definitions for common planning terms such as *activities, strategies, tasks, deliverables,* and so on. Almost any set of terms will work if you establish a clear definition of how you are using them up-front and share those definitions often and widely. For the sake of simplicity, I've chosen to paraphrase definitions from the online version of the *Online Dictionary for Library and Information Science* edited by Joan M. Reitz.

Goal: A general direction or aim that an organization commits itself to attain in order to further its mission; a goal is often expressed in abstract terms with no time limits

Strategy: The broader approach you use to achieve a goal

Objective: A specific achievable outcome of the actions taken to achieve a strategy

SMART Objectives: Objectives that are specific, measurable, achievable, realistic, and timely

Activities/Tasks/Deliverables: The steps, actions, or activities that are performed to achieve objectives

This discussion of terminology was not meant to undermine the importance of goals and objectives. Goals are critical in building buy-in for a large-scale project and for developing a shared understanding of what will be achieved. Experienced librarians, who want to understand your project, will look for its goals and objectives first.

No matter which large-scale project I have worked on, I have been surprised by how often I've had to justify the project at every stage of development, even when the goals seemed to be self-evident. For example, I was hired as a new director at Minitex to create an online e-book collection that would be available to all Minnesotans. While Minitex and the Minnesota State Library worked to launch this collection, called Ebooks Minnesota, I was repeatedly asked to justify the project, despite overwhelming, statewide demand for the service.

You will be explaining your project through every step of the process. It is best to accept this fact and use your goal statements to help sell the project. These statements can become something like an elevator pitch—short, clear, compelling statements. A project goal is a vivid statement of what the project will achieve and how patrons will benefit from it. One of the project goals for Ebooks Minnesota was: offer every library in Minnesota access to a large, no-cost, shared e-book collection.

To dive deeper into strategies, goals, and objectives, I recommend the book *Start with Why* by Simon Sinek, which should be mandatory reading for every library leader. For public libraries, *Strategic Planning for Results* by Sandra Nelson is an old standby, and is both solid and helpful. There are quite a few library planning books for academics; a recent title, *Strategic Planning for Academic Libraries*, from the University of Utah's staff, is a good beginner's guide.

GOALS ARE EASY, SCOPE IS HARD

Projects that do not have a Project Scope Statement are plagued with scope creep issues.

—PAUL BUREK

You developed a pre-scope statement earlier in your project; now it's time to create a full scope statement. *Scope* was defined in chapter 2 as the set of actions and the parameters you will work within to complete the project. Scope statements include the listing of items or tasks that need to be done in a certain time with the defined resources. Scope gets a lot of attention in project management literature. Defining the scope of your project required time and attention during the planning process. Like goal statements, a scope statement can be used as an elevator speech to help define your project.

If done correctly, scope limits a project manager's responsibility and authority to the key project targets. All projects have constraints, and scope can be an important place to clarify those constraints. The three common constraints are:

- Costs
- Time
- Available resources

These three constraints are often pictured as bubbles, and if you push on one bubble, it will impact the size and shape of the other two. How you balance these three constraints over the course of the project will become the matrix for how the project is judged by others.

There is a critically important reason you want to contain scope creep. James P. Lewis found that the major indicator of an at-risk project is the number of change requests coming in. If you talk to any experienced project manager, they will tell you horror stories about scope creep. I think of it as a hydra-like monster; if you cut off one head, two more will pop up. Catherine Elton, of the Project Management Institute, stated in 2018 that 52 percent of projects experience scope creep, a figure that was up significantly over the preceding five years. Scope creep is a real thing, and is not to be taken lightly.

As stated, scope creep happens when work gets added to a project after it is already defined and under way. A memorable experience I had with scope creep involved an e-book app development project. The project started with the goal of making a high-quality, limited-feature e-book reading app for public libraries, to help them grab control back from vendors. Two years into the project and from seemingly out of nowhere, discussions started on adding in millions of academic journal articles.

Project experts like Carly Wiggins Searcy have recommended that from day one, planning teams should define both what the scope of the project *is*, and what the scope of the project *is not*. As time goes on, the this-project-is-not list can be used to derail change requests before they gain political momentum. You should note, though, that there will be times when you'll need to expand the scope of your project for either practical or political reasons; if so, try to keep limits on that growth. The tighter you define the project's scope from the beginning, the better you will be able to eliminate or at least manage scope creep.

ACTIVITIES BY ANY OTHER NAME

Success in life is about project management. Determine deliverables, make milestones, and always pursue the critical path.

—RYAN LILLY

Activities is another one of those project management terms that can have many different names, such as tasks, actions, deliverables, action items (or action steps), and other terms linked to specific planning models. Again, it doesn't matter what you call these actions, just be consistent. Working on activities is where the details become focused. A concrete and comprehensive breakdown of specific tasks or actions is important because most librarians want a solid understanding of how the goals of the project will be achieved.

In enumerating the project's activities, you are providing a tangible vision of how the work will proceed. Once you have identified specific tasks or actions, you can then assign people, resources, and a time frame to achieve the activities, and crucially, you can sequence the activities into a logical order. You are answering questions like:

- What work will occur?
- How much work will be done?
- Who will carry out the work?
- How long will the work take and when can it be done?
- What resources are needed to do the work?

All project management software packages are designed to arrange a list of tasks into a sequence and identify needed resources within a specific, sequential time frame.

In laying out the tasks, the whole project becomes focused and many steps that might be missed can leap out at you. Tasks always have specific steps; for example, these are the step in a vendor demonstration schedule:

1. Develop a vendor requirement rubric by April 10.
2. Six, one-hour vendor demonstrations will take place on April 15–16 in the Acme conference room.
3. Committee members will score vendors according to the rubric by April 19.

4. The project steering committee will select a vendor by April 21.

5. Contract negotiation will be completed by May 1.

Several of these activities will have lengthy sub-steps. In the activities stage, make sure to include possible barriers to your activities and potential ways to remove those barriers. A barrier could be: you're not sure you can get all the vendors to show up on the two chosen dates. The plan should include alternate ways of removing barriers.

SCHEDULING AND RESOURCES

Failure to consider resource allocation in scheduling almost always leads to a schedule that cannot be achieved.

—JAMES P. LEWIS

A key part of a plan is the project schedule; this schedule lists specific tasks to complete, the time frame for each task, and who has the responsibility to achieve the task. Achievement milestones are also part of the project blueprint. For small projects, the project schedule along with a goal, outcomes, and budget may be all that is required. For large-scale initiatives, there are dozens of software and open-source scheduling tools that can facilitate the scheduling process.

Among the most common tools are critical path management (CPM), control diagrams (e.g., PERT charts), and Gantt charts. These tools focus on visual representations that can bring clarity and help with communication, while also revealing interdependencies and duplications among complex activities. The most valuable contribution of these tools is focusing on time-critical activities that cannot be ignored. Moreover, these tools are so commonly used in project management that not including them can appear to be a sign of incompetence.

The project schedule starts with a list of all activities that will be required to do the work. The list of activities will include time constraints and the resources (human, physical, and digital) required, as well as what must come before any given activity and what must follow. Two popular tools (CPM and PERT) visually display the schedule, which enhances communication and can highlight activities that are interdependent. It is common to find both of these visual tools used together.

Critical Path Management (CPM)

Critical path management allows for an estimation of the project's end date. The "critical path" is the shortest path required to complete the project, and thereby defines the minimum completion time for the entire project if *all* estimates are met. The focus is not on the number of activities, but on the total time for doing the needed activities in the correct sequence. Managers should pay attention to the project's critical activities as identified in CPM, as it will give the earliest notification of possible schedule slippage. It also reveals paths that have slack or the ability to absorb delays, which allows the project manager to refocus resources as needed to keep on schedule.

Program Evaluation and Control Technique (PERT)

PERT diagrams resemble a flow chart and show the relationships between tasks. They reveal the tasks which can move in more than one direction, and they make it easy to identify critical paths. PERT differs from CPM in that you can estimate the probability that an action will occur on schedule. In most large-scale library projects, you don't know exactly how long many activities will take. PERT lets you forecast a range of possible times to complete an activity. With PERT diagrams you can develop norms or probabilities for many complex activities. It can be time-consuming to create PERT charts, so give yourself time.

Gantt Charts

The *Encyclopedia of Management* claims that Gantt charts are the most widely used of all the scheduling tools. Indeed, the format will be familiar to most librarians and has been around for decades. Gantt charts are a visual aid that shows the major project tasks over a specific timeline and makes overlaps and deadlines clear to the reader. These charts are easy to read and are displayed as a table. The charts help provide structure while clarifying available resources within a specific time frame. In most such charts, *time* is on the horizontal axis and *resources* is on the vertical axis. Gantt charts allow a project manager to try out different schedules. Like PERT and CPM, Gantt charts are time-consuming to create, and they can take a lot of work to keep updated.

Project Management Software

It doesn't matter too much which [scheduling] package you select, as they all have strong and weak points.

—JAMES P. LEWIS

I have seen time and again that people confuse project management with project management software, probably because the software is more fun than dealing with the management process. I myself have made the mistake of jumping into putting content into a software package before having all the variables I needed. Most new project managers are likely to make this same mistake. (But perhaps you should do it wrong the first time so you can learn why you should do it right the next time.)

For smaller projects, many people cobble together different software packages like Slack, Dropbox, and Excel. Using a mix of software systems is also common in large-scale projects. Only organizations with a lot of authority can force the use of one controlling software system, and that's an uncommon scenario in libraries. A popular model in libraries is to use a communication package (Slack) with a scheduling system (Basecamp) and a separate document storage platform (Google Drive).

If you want to try to stay with one software package, you can. However, this is a fast-changing marketplace, so some of the early project management systems I used no longer exist. At this writing, Basecamp, Teamwork, Trello, Evernote, Hive, Jira, Smartsheet, and Microsoft Project are making the list of the best software. The open-source software that gets good reviews includes Project Libre, OpenProject, MyCollab, and GitLab. I could go on with these types of lists forever. Check the latest reviews and with your technology experts before you make a final choice.

CONTINGENCY PLANNING

Of major importance to the project is to identify the risks and determine how the team will address them.

—JERRY F. HEIMANN

The Project Management Institute defines *contingency planning* as having clear steps that you can take once a risk becomes a reality. In the corporate world, almost all project management plans include substantial risk management plans, especially with building projects. You need to identify possible risks and show options to deal with negative situations. In my opinion, it is best to include a contingency section within every major section of your plan, rather than have a separate contingency plan. But, frankly, both approaches work. In most cases, library project plans, other than those for new buildings, do not have lengthy risk sections, which is regrettable. The main point in contingency planning is to demonstrate awareness of potential problems before they occur and show you have thought through methods of dealing with problematic situations.

BUDGETS

The budget evolved from a management tool into an obstacle to management.

—CHARLES EDWARDS

Project management budgets include items like labor, equipment, software, space, human resources, operating costs, and insurance. You will be trying to estimate costs throughout the entire project and specifically for each phase of development. The budget is not a static document; it will change as you learn more and as circumstances change. It's best to use a numbering scheme to show iterations of the budget over time. I typically ran two budgets. One was the messy, working budget with all the details and projections. In this working budget, I ran projections and alternative scenarios. My second budget was mostly the same numbers, but I had simplified, organized, and cleaned it up to present to governing bodies and other outsiders. It's more work to run two budgets, but after you present a messy budget full of contingencies and best guesses to a governing body, you won't want to do it again.

Delving into the work activities and the human resources department will give you most of your budget details. You will probably be getting preliminary estimates from vendors that you can use for budget estimating purposes, knowing that there will be a request for proposal (RFP) process or an equivalent process ahead that will give you the final numbers. Your budget is always an estimate even if you have exact price quotes. In every project, things happen that will impact the costs that you didn't anticipate. Make sure you build in generous contingency funds for the unknowns.

In many ways, managing a project budget is a lot like managing any library budget. While dated, Hallam and Dalston's *Managing Budgets and Finances: A How-to-Do-It Manual for Librarians and Information Professionals* is an excellent resource for in-depth information about budgeting. You should also consider finding an experienced budget manager to be one of your advisors.

COMMUNICATION PLAN

The single biggest problem in communication is the illusion that it has taken place.

—GEORGE BERNARD SHAW

It is difficult to underestimate the importance of a communication plan. When you are working at a large scale, librarians want to be informed, particularly if they are excited about the initiative. Many problems can be forestalled if there is open and frequent communication with everyone. A communication plan includes who needs to be informed, which communication tools you will use, when reports are due, plans for keeping the public informed, and updates of successes achieved and difficulties encountered.

A communication strategy will include various written and verbal tools to share information at both the formal and informal levels. In a study by Matt Lee and myself conducted in 2015, we found that library consortium managers were increasingly frustrated in attempting to communicate with participants. It is likely that communication will be the most criticized part of your project, since it is nearly impossible to do it perfectly. The best advice is to use a variety of communication tools and repeat messages frequently.

The Lee and Horton study found the following communication tools used most often in collaborative projects:

- *E-mail:* Despite numerous predictions of the death of e-mail, it remains one of the most commonly used and effective communication channels. The main advantage I have found with e-mail is that it creates a backtrail so you can prove the information was shared if someone questions it later.
- *E-mail lists:* Many project management software packages include the ability to create lists of people who will be interested in specific parts

of your project. For instance, when launching a statewide publishing platform, we had one e-mail list for academic librarians, one for public librarians, and another for the authors, contest judges, and so on.

- *Shared document sites*: Shared document sites have two important uses. They allow your participants to find files (minutes, agenda, plans) in one place, while at the same time they serve as a way to document your project over time. There are numerous online shared-site resources. I have had success with the Google suite, Basecamp, SharePoint, and Dropbox.
- *Web conferencing and video-conferencing tools*: Zoom, Bluejeans, GoTo-Meeting, and other online conferencing tools are more widely used now than when we conducted the study, since they have proven invaluable during the pandemic.
- *Communities of interest (COIs)*: You may be able to establish self-governing communities of interest for certain aspects of your project. These COIs give those who are genuinely interested a chance to interact within the community and with the project team. We found these COIs to be most effective for academic libraries, but they have value in public libraries and user communities as well.

General communication tools:

- *Online newsletters*: These tend to be used for more formal communication and are intended for a wider, and often less involved, audience.
- *Websites*: While often tedious to maintain if the project is large, you will need a website. It may be of marginal use to those deeply involved in the project, but it will be the first source of information for potential adopters. Check out the Library Publishing Coalition's website as an example of how a web page can be an asset to a relatively new organization. Many library project websites serve as a document-sharing site and have embedded, securely locked sections with information for the project's participants.
- *Social media*: Facebook, Twitter, YouTube, and Instagram are among the most heavily used social media sites for the general population; librarians also tend to be heavy Twitter usage. For example, the New York Public Library has well over 2.5 million Twitter followers.
- *Webinars*: These are an excellent way to share information in a controlled manner, while allowing questions and other interactions.

- *Conference programs*: I've found these to be one of the most effective communication channels for sharing information about large projects. You get to make a face-to-face pitch, answer questions, and be available after the talk for more in-depth discussions. When we launched the Minnesota Libraries Publishing Project, we had a pool of 10 people who made presentations at more than 20 events. We all shared our slide decks and modified the decks to fit each audience.
- *One-on-one conversations*: Whether they are face-to-face, phone, by individual e-mail, or by text, don't forget the importance of direct communication to individuals. It can take an enormous amount of time, but you need a place for the personal touch.

Once you've decided how you're going to communicate, the next question is who will do the communicating. I recommend not having the project manager be the main communicator. The project manager should be used for critical announcements when you want people to pay attention. Let others send out day-to-day messages, and save the project manager's voice for times when it needs to be noticed.

LAUNCHING, MAINTAINING, ASSESSING, AND HANDOVERS

No plan, no control.

—JAMES P. LEWIS

You will need to roughly sketch out how you think the project launch will go and how the system will be maintained after the launch. At this point, these can be brief sections with indications of when they will be expanded and discussed later in fuller format with the governing body. Before starting a project, it can be difficult to state how you will close it out and turn it over to the maintenance group. Handover decisions are always decided by the governing group, so writing this part of the plan can be tricky.

The handover part of the project that you need to fully develop is assessment. If you are evaluating your project process and your delivered system correctly, you will have to build in the assessment tools and techniques you will need as the project goes along. You also need to know which matrixes will be used to evaluate the project process so you know what you will be judged on at the end.

IN CONCLUSION, DOUBTERS ALWAYS DOUBT

Plans are worthless. Planning is essential.

—DWIGHT D. EISENHOWER

There were several things I wish I could have communicated better to my staff when I was an academic library director. One of these was the true value of planning. It always seemed to me that many of my staff either thought planning would solve everything exactly as they personally wanted it, or that planning was useless and would solve nothing.

In veering toward these extremes of planning, many people missed one of its major benefits. It is not the final plan that is all-important. The value of planning lies in the conversations that open up as you go through the planning process; it is during those conversations that people learn what they need to know, can hunt for new ways of doing things, and discover options that open up possibilities for better solutions. Going through a planning process gives people a chance to stop and look at the big picture and make some crucial decisions.

Planning is integral to project management. Given the temporary nature of projects, the plan's work activities, timeline, and resource identification become critical to achieving the project goals. When working at scale, there is no way to marshal the forces needed to make significant progress without a clear blueprint to follow. As Eisenhower said, there will be changes that occur as you start implementing your plan. We will discuss those in the next chapter.

REFERENCES

Books24x7, Inc, and Project Management Institute. *A guide to the Project Management Body of Knowledge (Pmbok guide), fourth edition.* 4th ed. Newtown Square, Pa: Project Management Institute, 2008.

Elton, Catherine. "Scope Patrol." *PM Network* 32 (July 2018): 38–45.

Hallam, Arlita, and Teresa R. Dalston. *Managing Budgets and Finances: A How-to-Do-It Manual for Librarians and Information Professionals.* New York: Neal-Schuman, 2005.

Lee, Matt, and Valerie Horton. "Communication in Library Consortia." *Collaborative Librarianship* 7 (2015): 5–12.

Nelson, Sandra S. *Strategic Planning for Results.* New Delhi: Indian Publishing House, 2009.

Reitz, Joan M., ed. *Online Dictionary for Library and Information Science: ODLIS.* Westport, CT: Libraries Unlimited, 2005.

Searcy, Carly Wiggins. *Project Management in Libraries: On Time, On Budget, On Target.* Chicago: American Library Association, 2018.

Sinek, Simon. *Start with Why: How Great Leaders Inspire Everyone to Take Action.* New York: Portfolio, 2009.

Thompson, Gregory C., Harish Maringanti, Rick Anderson, Catherine B. Soehner, and Alberta Comer. *Strategic Planning for Academic Libraries: A Step-by-Step Guide.* Chicago: American Library Association, 2019.

EIGHT

THE SUBTLE ART OF WOOING

PRESENTATION IS EVERYTHING

A leader needs to be able to articulately and passionately outline a vision.

—GILLIAN M. MCCOMBS

We have moved from the planning stage into the executing stage of the project management process. Your plan is written, you've captured mountains of details and created shiny charts and graphs to wow your readers. Now is the time to sell your plan. You need to look for that inner passionate voice that Gillian McCombs recommends. The execution stage is the moment where your participants and stakeholder will have expectations that must be met by your plan. Most people will be introduced to your project as you present the plan for it. How you deliver that plan will go far in creating the impression of the entire project. You're going to get to show others how your project's outcomes will either improve the library or transform patrons' lives, and if you're lucky, it will do both.

GOING PUBLIC

They may forget what you said, but they will never forget how you made them feel.

—CARL W. BUECHNER

Presenting the project plan to the governing authority, stakeholders, and potential participants is a transformational moment. It can be nerve-wracking because this step is one of the moments when large projects are derailed, or worse, killed off. You'll need to put a lot of thought and preparation into your plan presentation strategy. You should use your team of informal advisors and experts to help you polish the plan and your presentation strategy.

In your presentation, remember to start with a strong, compelling vision. Nobody commits to massive actions and capital outlays if they are not inspired by how things will be changed for better after your project is completed. You will be doing some kind of in-person presentations, but the foundation of your talks will come from the planning document. The participants will have expectations of what they will find in a planning document, so in both your written and oral presentations, you must deliver.

Final Planning Report

Your final planning report should include work plans, timelines, finances, resources needed, project organization, personnel, and risks. It probably will be an extended version of the preliminary plan. You'll be presenting charts and graphs that illustrate your timeline and work plan. These need to be professionally polished. Some sections can still be labeled as a "draft" or by some other wording indicating that you anticipate things will change as time goes on. Your planning process probably revealed several issues that hadn't been anticipated in the ideation stage. Make sure you reveal that information up front. Also, present any unexpected pluses and potential minuses that were uncovered during the research.

Many large libraries and organizations already have templates for submitting formal proposals. You can adapt one of those, or you can use one of the dozens of templates and planning tools that are available online from the Project Management Institute and other sources. Your final plan will expand upon the following categories from your preliminary planning document and include a few new sections as well:

- *Background and Purpose*: Describe the purpose of the project and define the outcomes that will make the project worthwhile. Part of this section can include the project description, which is a concise, short description of your project. This description can become your elevator speech and be used to introduce the project in what will undoubtedly be many public meetings to follow. Given how important a concise project description is during the life of the project, I recommend spending a lot of time polishing it.

- *Project Scope*: What are the boundaries of the project? What is included and excluded from this project? Some experts recommend a discussion of what is out-of-scope for the project. They argue that this can help manage expectations, set limits, and reduce scope creep. I have never used this technique myself, but it makes sense, and you should consider it.
- *Intended Audience*: This section can include both internal users (library staff) and external users (patrons) and should be closely tied to project outcomes.
- *Project Outcomes*: Who will benefit from the work being done? How will they be changed? How will the participating libraries be improved? You could consider combining this section with a description of success measures, but make sure you separate the outcomes (items that change for the better) and the outputs (usage or other statistics).
- *Project Sponsors*: What is the governing body overseeing the project? How are they exercising that authority during the project implementation stage? This is typically the entity that has the authority to sign contracts and control overall funding.
- *Stakeholders and Reviewers*: With large-scale projects, there is likely to be a sizable group of participating libraries or other organizations. It is not uncommon to have some stratification among the participants, often based on their level of commitment. This can be a good place to mention your initial thoughts on increasing participation in the project over time.
- *Decision-Making Authority*: Decision-making authority can be combined with the "Project Sponsor" section or pulled out separately, depending on how you want to emphasize authority and responsibility in the project's reporting relationships.
- *Project Manager*: The person(s) responsible for overseeing the project and keeping it on schedule and budget. Typically, the project manager reports directly to the project sponsors.
- *Project Leadership Team*: This tends to be a small group that works with the project manager on the daily execution of the project tasks. It may or may not be too early to include specific names, but role definitions should be included.

- *Team or Committee Structure*: With large-scale library projects, there may be many project teams that come and go. Include a team charge for each group along with its reporting relationships. In libraries, it is common to use the term *committees* for long-standing teams and the term *task forces* for short-term tasks. However, your choice of nomenclature doesn't matter, though you might be surprised how much some people care about topics like this. You might want to use the terminology used by your largest stakeholder. Whatever you choose, be consistent.
- *Project Timeline*: Include the project's start and stop dates as well as its major milestones. Graphics pay back dividends at this stage, especially when presented in conjunction with explanatory text. The charts are likely to be combed over by stakeholders, so go for professional quality even if it means paying for a design firm to produce the final copy.
- *Resources*: Provide an overview of the human, technical, physical, and financial resources needed to complete the project. This section may be where you include risks and threats to the project. Note: threats are going to fall into either political or resource-based categories, and you may want to handle these differently.
- *Communication Plan*: You can include this plan in the main document or treat it as a separate document, depending on how much attention you want to draw to it.
- *Budget*: Share a big-picture financial snapshot that includes staff resources, costs, and other critical resources needed to complete the project. Include funding sources.
- *Action Lists*: This section gives your workflows and timetables as spelled out in your Gantt, CPM, PERT, or equivalent charts. The goal is to lay out in detail the steps and stages of the project's work to potential stakeholders and approvers.
- *Risk Factors*: Risk, as defined at this level, is an assessment of potential threats that could jeopardize the project, including threats to funding, technology, vendor availability, or online security. One advantage of including a risk analysis this early in the project is that it shows your stakeholders that though you are optimistic, you are also aware of the inherent risks in doing large-scale initiatives.
- *Long-Term Viability*: You will probably not be expected to lay out complete plans for the long-term survival of your project until after it has actually been launched. That said, it is a good idea to summarize discussions

and current thinking on the project's long-term viability, as well as your intention to fully flesh out this section later.

- *Related Issues*: Include any special features or issues related to your specific situation.

Finally, when it comes to final plans, size doesn't matter. As Winston Churchill said, "This report, by its very length, defends itself against the risk of being read." I've been in a lot of discussions about the correct length for a planning document. No doubt, brevity sells better. My recommendation is to make the report the length it needs to be. Then include a substantial executive summary for those not inclined to read the entire document.

ONE LAST GUT-CHECK

The truth of the matter is that you always know the right thing to do. The hard part is doing it.

—NORMAN SCHWARZKOPF

The decision to move forward on a project is a complicated one. Obviously, in the end, the governing authority will make the final decision on whether the initiative is a go or not. But before you get that approval, take a moment and think about the commitment you are going to make to this project. Is it truly the right thing to do? Is it the right thing for *you* specifically to do?

You and your team will have just gone through a significant planning process, where you looked at the benefits to be gained from your project and assessed the risks of failure. Throughout the planning process, you were asking—is this a good idea? Is it bold enough? Will librarians want to join in? It is a mental juggling act to be an enthusiastic salesperson for your project while being a clear-eyed realist about the possibility of success.

Take some time and seriously decide whether you want to continue the project. Once, I did a lengthy analysis of whether my library should sign up to do beta testing for a new online catalog system. There was a lot of sizzle around the project, and having my library agree to be a beta-level tester would have given us a lot of street credibility. If successful, the catalog had the potential to move our patron services to a whole new level. But during the analysis, details kept coming up which made me increasingly uncomfortable, until it reached a point that I ended up recommended we not join. My superiors and colleagues were shocked, since I had put hundreds of hours of my and the staff's time into the analysis. I explained my reasoning and everyone agreed. I was a relatively new librarian at the time and was terrified that I had damaged my reputation by not recommending going forward.

It turned out that it was the right decision. That beta catalog system failed and disappeared without ever having reached full production, and I had made a reputation for myself as being thoughtful. The next big, risky project I recommended went through without political wrangling. I can't say the same will happen to you, but I do recommend that you be willing to pull the plug if the evidence gained during the planning process says that your project isn't what you hoped it would be.

Take the time to know what your values are before launching a new project. Having gone through this self-reflection, you will find that when you go on to cheerlead for your project, you will be speaking with an authentic voice that can motivate others.

THE ART AND SCIENCE OF WOOING

If you can't explain it simply, you don't understand it well enough.

—ALBERT EINSTEIN

At this point, you've made your decision to move forward and it's time to sell this puppy to others. Among the definitions of the word *woo* in the dictionary is "the act of seeking to persuade a group or person to do something." That definition works when you're trying to launch a large-scale library initiative. However, the primary definition of *woo*—seeking the favor of someone—also fits. You want people to fall in love with your project and share the experience with you.

David Burkus has researched why great ideas fail. He found that only 20 of 4,400 patents for improved mousetraps ever saw the light of day. Burkus argues that truly creative ideas are, by definition, a rejection of the status quo, and this makes humans inherently uncomfortable. A part of humanity might long for creative and innovative ideas, but we also crave certainty and structure. Burkus argues that for a great idea to be adopted it must be new, remarkable, and over-the-top useful.

As you develop your presentation to sell your project, you should be thinking of ways to address your listeners' fear and biases. A powerful technique is to answer potential concerns before they are asked. Take the time to identify each of your stakeholders' primary concerns, fears, or biases before presenting your plan, and then have your answers ready. Turn to your advisors for insight into how people will react to your project proposal; use your planning team and informal advisors to test the effectiveness of both your plan and how you will present it. Feedback is your friend.

We discussed Everett M. Rogers's "diffusion of innovation" theory earlier. Rogers's research identified the stages in technology adoption, but he also focused on what caused an idea to spread. He identified five key factors:

1. *Relative advantage*: The new product is better than the current option. The better the new product is over the one it is replacing, the higher will be the rate of adoption. Think of how much better flip phones were over landline phones.
2. *Compatibility*: Do people have past knowledge of or experience with the new idea or product? The more similar the concept is to existing norms, the better the chance of adoption.
3. *Complexity*: How difficult will it be for people to understand the new idea or use the new product? Is it simple to explain?
4. *Trialability*: Is it easy to test the new product? How many barriers are there between the user and the product? It may be easy to use, but is it easy to play with and learn about? Pay attention to these potential barriers, since they have killed off a lot of potentially good library systems.
5. *Observability*: Are other librarians successfully using the new idea or product? High visibility by library influencers and thought-leaders can be critical to pushing adoption.

When you present your planning document to the wider world, check to see if you have considered Rogers's points. Answering the questions people have before they even realize they have them can go a long way toward wooing people to your idea.

Wooing the Leadership Team

The strength of collective decision-making and political responsibility is not only a question of recognizing other people's abilities. It is also recognizing one's limitations.

—ARUNA ROY

One of the biggest decisions you make might *not* be one you're even conscious of making. Have you thought out what kind of relationship you want with your leadership team or steering committee? The ideal is to have a close, honest, open relationship with them where everything is discussed, team members have each other's back, and everyone is pulling in the same direction. In the library world, this is common but not universal. Large library initiatives are inherently political, and politics is complicated.

It's worth your time to plan carefully for those first critical meetings with that most important group, your leadership team. Take a minute and decide how you're going to discuss sensitive issues with these close coworkers. What is your strategy on how you're going to treat this group? Will they be your sounding board when you're unsure about something? Or will you bring them mostly completed decisions and just ask for tweaks and approval? There is a big difference between those two ends of the spectrum, and each one has pros and cons. Your political situation may indicate which option you choose.

It is not uncommon for a planning committee to morph into a steering committee (or leadership team) when a project is approved. You will be spending a lot of time with your planning/steering committee. I recommend starting with one-on-one meetings with every member before the first group meeting, and continuing those one-on-ones as the project progresses. You need to make sure you're hearing everything you need to know. Planning team members are your best conduit into the wider world.

If you are new to team management, you can take online courses on how to run meetings, how to do group facilitation, and understand team dynamics. A neutral coach can be a sounding board and support system, so it may be worth paying for a coach out of your own pocket if need be. Setting up the groundwork to have a good relationship with the leadership team will pay off in countless ways.

If you are lucky enough to have a leadership team you trust, then consider using a true group decision-making model. Sharing decision-making can be both helpful and powerful. Let the group make the tough decisions, and you'll have both their buy-in and someone to share the blame with if things go wrong. A group brings more information into the decision-making process. More views, more political nuances, more talent, and a broader perspective will come from working with a trusted, close-knit group. If you are lucky enough to have this dynamic, you can trust your decision-making with a much higher degree of confidence than if you make the decisions alone.

Wooing Stakeholders

There's more to a pitch than a big presentation and a yea-or-nay decision . . . You should carefully lay a foundation for your argument, tactic by tactic.

—SUSAN ASHFORD AND JAMES DETERT

There is a critical step during large-scale library initiatives where you get the buy-in of your stakeholders and an official agreement to launch by your governing authority, which could be the same group or a separate one. It's common to use the same selling techniques and presentations to both groups. How you woo these groups depends on the politics of your project. If your project is a shared online catalog, for example, you probably will need some ancillary, unofficial buy-in from library staff who will be heavily impacted by the change. If your project is developing a new library app, you'll need the buy-in of sponsoring organizations, funders, and probably the information technology department as well. If your project is a statewide, self-publishing book platform, you'll need buy-in by book support groups like the Center for the Book, the state library, and a statewide consortium if one exists. It will all depend on the circumstances. But you will need to obtain final buy-in from a diverse group of people.

If you are a mid-level manager, it can be difficult to get buy-in from those higher up the chain of command. Most first-time project managers are mid-level managers. This type of obstacle has long been recognized in business circles, and the concept of "issue selling" was developed to address it. In 2015, Susan Ashford and James Detert examined decades of research to look at what techniques were the most successful ones for the mid-level manager to use within a hierarchy. They found that those managers who were most successful used

- substantial preparation
- high-quality visuals
- carefully considered timing

The successful mid-level managers also employed skills like strong arguments, political awareness, and existing relationships to support their efforts.

As you plan your wooing strategy, first consider what you're selling. Ashford and Detert found that pitches tailored to specific audiences were the most effective ones. You need to customize your pitch to meet the political and aspirational needs of your audience. Ask yourself what motivates your superiors, what do they value, and what pressures are they under? If you can pitch your new service or product to match both the organization's and your superiors' needs, you are more likely to gain support.

According to Ashford and Detert, the second most effective strategy was to frame the issue in context. Your new project will be one of three things:

1. A new product or service to help patrons
2. An improvement to an existing product, service, or process
3. A way to improve the work of library employees

It also may be some combination of these, so choose the most compelling argument. Use the strongest frame to locate your pitch. For instance, if you are pitching an improved service, you could give estimates that demonstrate the potential for increased efficiencies. Customize your pitch to the needs of your listeners.

Ashford and Detert found that other techniques could help a pitch, including

- involving others, especially thought-leaders or movers and shakers
- acknowledging existing organizational or cultural norms
- assuring compliance with existing organizational values and ways of operations in order to foster a sense of competence and continuation of the status quo (note: this option may require a lot of finesse)
- getting the timing right to match with the organization's goals

There will be times when you need to do substantial cultural preparation before the timing is right to sell an idea. With some of my former superiors, I found that if I pitched an idea and then didn't bring it up again for several months, that idea had magically morphed into their idea. And who cares who gets the credit for the idea? You just want to get the job done. You should consider your ethics, but in the end, you are trying to do the greatest good possible.

Finally, you should recognize that wooing is an ongoing process that requires communication and patience on your part. My personal experience suggests that helping stakeholders or governing board members see their role in the project went a long way to building support. Those listening to your pitch will probably have two questions:

- How will this impact my organization?
- How will it impact me personally?

Make sure you address both questions. Superiors have to consider their own reputation and political standing when making decisions. You do that too, don't you? Remember, we are all about improving the services and products we provide to our patrons, so leading with values, impact, and outcomes can never be wrong.

Community Buy-in

The brain doesn't pay attention to boring things.

—JOHN MEDINA

Your work during the ideation stage was the first step in getting buy-in from the community. Your ongoing communication about the project was the second step. Communication is just as necessary for buy-in from the community as it is for getting approval from the governing authority. The tools you have for communicating with the public include conference presentations, conversations, blog or newsletter posts, web pages, e-mails, texting, webinars, articles, and social media posts.

One of your most powerful communication vehicles is your network of advisors, friends, and colleagues, and the library administrators you've recruited to be your mouthpiece into the greater community. This can be a formal relationship—look at the DPLA's ambassador program as an example—or it can be a private agreement between you, your leadership team, and their circle of contacts. Everett Rogers found that tapping into ever-widening circles of connections is the most effective tool available to help speed the adoption of a new technology.

I used the term "you" here, but this shouldn't just be you; it should also be your colleagues, your planning or steering team, your governance members, your stakeholders, and your employees. You should be sharing messages that are amplified by your in-groups. Your presentations should be recorded and loaded onto a streaming video site, your slide decks should be loaded onto SlideShare or a similar slide sharing platform, and your blog or website should be making it all available as well. Have a team of people making presentations; this will significantly broaden your reach.

Another tool that can come in handy at this point is the road show. You and your team should spend some part of your time on the road talking and listening to the library community. This is a time for building relationship-based support, gathering data, and providing a public face for your big project. There will be questions out there that can only be answered in person. You need to identify key internal and external stakeholders in each locality and talk to them. Talk about the nitty-gritty details, ask their advice, and make them feel part of something new and exciting. Asking questions and then listening to people's answers is a powerful tool. A tip: brush up on your active listening skills.

PRE-MORTEMS

Great leaders have "productive paranoia"—they're always considering how things could go wrong.

—ALEXANDER LAUFER ET AL.

Risk management is the process of identifying, quantifying, and analyzing specific threats to a project. Project management literature, particularly that associated with building projects, focuses heavily on risk management. I recommend Tom Kendrick's *Identifying and Managing Project Risk* if you're looking for a deep dive into the topic. My preferred risk assessment technique is the "pre-mortem."

The opposite of a postmortem, a pre-mortem is a type of early risk assessment. It may seem odd to look at your project as if it were dead before you've even begun, but that's the best time to do it. A pre-mortem determines what can go wrong early on and can help you design your project to avoid or overcome those problems.

There is something about the pre-mortem technique that helps clarify participants' thinking in this thought exercise. If you are concerned that people will not express their reservations about a project, this technique is tailored to make it safe and oddly fun for those with concerns to express them. By using "prospective hindsight," or imagining a future event as if it has already happened, you can increase the likelihood that you will identify potential threats ahead of time.

Pre-mortems have been found to help eliminate biases, groupthink, and overconfidence in planning teams. The process is not complicated. Your team envisions what plausible ways the project dies six months out, a year out, and so on. A common method of doing a pre-mortem uses these five steps:

1. Make sure everyone on the team is fully aware of the project plan.
2. The leader announces that the project has failed, and everyone has a few minutes to imagine and write down the newspaper headline about that failure on separate index cards. Attendees are encouraged to write down things that normally wouldn't be considered or which could be considered impolitic.
3. The cards are anonymously shared and grouped, and duplicate headlines are eliminated.
4. The cards are ranked to focus on the most likely threats or weaknesses that caused the project to fail. A level of danger should be assigned to each potential threat and should be used to prioritize the development of potential solutions.
5. Small groups can be assigned to look at ways to guard against the threats and bring their solutions back to the next meeting.

During a large project, I typically reviewed the pre-mortem list with the leadership team every two months or so. We checked the status of the most significant threats and looked to see if others had developed.

Risk assessment is a balancing act. If you give the topic too much consideration, it can scare some participants away. If you give it too little, you show a lack of knowledge and experience. Moreover, you are taking a big risk in not developing contingency plans for potential threats. Make sure you run the risk assessment section of your final plan through your leadership team and your expert advisors. You want other opinions on this topic.

HUNTING FOR THOSE ELUSIVE RESOURCES

Being a Project Manager is like being an artist; you have the different colored process streams combining into a work of art.

—GREG CIMMARRUSTI

There are as many different ways of funding large-scale library projects as there are large-scale projects. It's difficult to break funding sources into logical groupings, since each project has its own internal logic, largely based on the project's governance structure and potential participants. A library project manager may be required to find resources, partners, grants, or those ever-elusive donors. Other managers may have the funding handled entirely by the governance infrastructure or some hybrid of the two. That said, there are several different funding models available.

Self-funded: The organization or several organizations fund the project out of their existing budgets. This model is common, particularly with shared catalog launches.

Philanthropic: In this model, large philanthropic organizations step in to fund a new venture. In some cases, major charitable organizations provide funding to a library project. The DPLA was largely created by funding from organizations like the Knight Foundation, the Bill and Melinda Gates Foundation, the Andrew W. Mellon Foundation, and the Alfred P. Sloan Foundation.

Member contributions: This is probably the most common model. The members of a consortium may contribute staff time, money, and physical or technological resources like building space, networks, software, or access to server farms. This model differs from self-funded models because the members are usually contributing relatively small fees, and there can be many members; look at the Library Publishing Coalition model as an example. The members' financial contributions can be one-time funds or ongoing contributions over several years, and sometimes they are a combination. The members' staff can be assigned to help a project on top of their existing duties, or be assigned away from their current work part- or full-time to work on the project.

State and local funding: This model has been used successfully for many decades. For instance, in Colorado, we used state funding along with federal grants to launch AspenCat, a shared Koha-based online catalog used by more than 100 small libraries statewide.

Consortium: Large projects can be funded out of a consortium's existing budget or can be funded by additional resources added to support the new project. Sometimes these projects stay within the original consortium, and sometimes they break away to form a second organization as the project matures.

Crowdsourcing or fundraising: I have never seen this model succeed for large-scale library initiatives. I could envision it as successful if it is used to pay for a planning process or some other small component of a larger project, though.

Hybrid: Many projects move through jaw-dropping convolutions of the above options. An example of this is SimplyE, an open-source e-book app. SimplyE was born in the New York Public Library, and that august library contributed millions to the project. After a time, they sought both federal grants and contributing partners. At Minitex, I wrote a successful federal grant for $1.2 million to support the app's development and assigned several of our programmers to code for it. Partners came and went over time, and the project eventually moved to a new home at the LYRASIS academic consortium, where more grants, membership fees, and usage fees helped pay for further development.

For many long-term projects, movement into a consortium home is common and stabilizing. However, hybrid funding is common for every large-scale collaborative initiative I have ever worked on. Finding funding can be complex and more like an art than a science. If major fundraising is part of your project manager's duties, you will probably need a strong second-in-command to take on many of the day-to-day management tasks of the project.

SOLD!

Time is a commodity that we always need more of desperately, but there is never enough of it.

—LINH TRAN

I've chosen to talk about timing your wooing in this final section of the chapter because timing is both nebulous and potentially one of the biggest threats to your library project. You can do everything right: you've communicated like a pro, developed key relationships, wooed stakeholders and funders, and generated excitement. Moreover, you may have created a plan that is a marvel of careful analysis and promising outcomes that will improve our profession while making a true difference in the lives of your patrons and your community. However, for all of that, *if the timing isn't right, none of that good work matters!*

This lesson is one of the most painful ones I ever had to learn. I worked hard to get a project off the ground, laying the foundation for months, doing research, and building a network. Then the 2008–2009-recession happened, and all state funding disappeared from my partner libraries, which had to start slashing their budgets. My beautiful idea died that day. I mourned it. While I never resurrected that project, other worthy large-scale initiatives came around eventually. You may have to walk away from a project you love, but I hope this doesn't happen to you.

The other important aspect of timing is finding the right time to raise your idea. If the largest library among your participants loses its director or is involved in a crisis, then it is a wise project manager who slows things down and waits for the right moment to push for project approval. Keep an eye on the trends and events in the profession as you move towards getting the final go-ahead to start your project. You might have to adjust to external circumstances.

In closing, Carly Wiggins Searcy states, "the meaningful part of project management is not creating charts or writing plans. It's the conversations, the transparency, the negotiation, and the collaborative problem solving that are required to create the right result . . . If you apply the skills, tools, and techniques outlined in this book while practicing responsibility, respect, fairness, and honesty, you will have better project outcomes." No one could say it better than that.

REFERENCES

Ashford, Susan J., and James Detert. "Get the Boss to Buy In: Learn to Sell Your Ideas up the Chain of Command." *Harvard Business Review* 93 (2015): 72–79.

Burkus, David. "Why Great Ideas Get Rejected: And How to Keep Yours from Being Shot Down." *Leader to Leader* 75 (2015): 50–55.

Kendrick, Tom. *Identifying and Managing Project Risk: Essential Tools for Failure-Proofing Your Project.* 3rd ed. New York: American Management Association, 2015.

Klein, Gary. "Performing a Project Premortem." *Harvard Business Review* 85 (2007): 18–19.

McCombs, Gillian M. "Abraham Lincoln, Management Guru! Lessons for Library Leadership on Resilience, True Grit, and Bouncing Forward." *portal: Libraries and the Academy* 13 (2013): 227–31.

Rogers, Everett M. *Diffusion of Innovations.* 5th ed. New York: Free Press, 2003.

NINE

HERDING CATS AND OTHER TEAM FAIRY TALES

A FRANK DISCUSSION

"The "P" in PM is as much about "people" management as it is about "project" management.

—CORNELIUS FICHTNER

In magical libraryland, people get along, there are no personality issues, and everyone suppresses their *own* agenda to achieve greater goals. The reason I love our profession is that I've seen this happy occurrence play out many times. Those who joined with me in large-scale initiatives were always intelligent, motivated, creative, and hard-working, and on some occasions, they were easy to work with. Unfortunately, these pleasant memories are not *always* associated with my project management work.

One of my library heroes, George Machovec, wrote about the difficulties of library collaboration. He said, "naysayers who habitually express negative or pessimistic views can be damaging to any collaborative effort." Machovec is particularly concerned with the impact of large geographic distances on group cohesiveness, and he worries that quieter personalities will not be heard in online groups. He is also concerned about the loss of social capital and trust-building in long-distance groups.

Jeremy Atkinson identified several barriers to successful collaboration. He looked at cultural dissimilarities and differences in work practices.

Staff who are resistant to change may be even more intransigent in collaborative situations. It's hard to ask people to work outside of their normal, comfortable expectations and professional boundaries; some will flourish in the situation, but not everyone will. Moreover, staff can have legitimate fears that they will be asked to take on new collaborative duties without a reduction in their current workload. Competing priorities are a constant issue in collaborative work. In fact, given the realities of library workloads, it is amazing how much work gets done cooperatively overall.

Some personalities may be difficult to manage in a collaborative work situation. Dominant or abrasive personalities may be accommodated at their home institution but can become disruptive in a new collaborative effort, where everyone is trying to figure out how to work together. Sometimes the negative impact of difficult personalities can be mitigated by effective communication, and sometimes not. Misunderstood expectations may be the unseen force behind some personnel problems.

When first seeing difficulties, the project manager should put on a deerstalker hat and see if they can figure out the underlying dynamic. Unfortunately, the reality is that not everyone has the best interests of the group at heart, though in my experience, that's rare in our profession. Often the only solution is to remove a problem personality from the team. Try to retain the right to be able to remove unsuccessful collaborators from your teams; and if you can't, do what all library managers are forced to do, and try to minimize and isolate problem people.

Most collaborative efforts come with a built-in expectation that the local institution will be giving up some level of autonomy or local control. I have heard many librarians explain how their cataloging, reference, customer service—or any library function you want—is so much better than the ones in their peer institutions. In general, this is not a problem, since it's a sign of professional pride in local work. In a collaborative, however, the new norms may not match local expectations, and this can cause genuine hardship for staff who must give up cherished beliefs and preferences.

Some obstacles that will inevitably come your way are unique to the management of a large-scale initiatives. The good news is that knowing about universal problems gives you time to prepare your arguments and resources in advance. You're going to need that quick elevator speech that tells people what your project is and why they should care in as few words as possible. But you will also need to have ready answers to the following questions:

- Why is your project so expensive?
- Why is everyone in your project fighting all the time?
- Why is your project going so slow?
- Why isn't Library A participating?
- Why did you let Library B participate?
- Why did Library C leave the project before it even launched?
- Why did you miss that deadline or milestone?

You get the idea. Be prepared to answer fair and unfair questions. Know in advance you will get unfair comments and questions will help you respond from a place of calm.

Facing conflict head-on is difficult but will ultimately lead to better outcomes if you are prepared and know in advance what criticism is going to occur. You need to have your internal reactions mapped out and have practiced your responses in advance. Think about how you react to setbacks. Can you face belligerent challenges with measured answers? Remember that pre-planning your answers and emotional responses to potential problems will make facing them easier.

Having a pool of advisors, coaches, and experienced project managers to guide you through the tough times ahead is also helpful. Above all, you should remember that project management is often problem management, and nothing you are facing hasn't been faced by generations of project managers before you. Take heart, this experience is going to teach you a lot!

TRUST AND OTHER TOUCHY-FEELY STUFF

In order to win a man to your cause, Lincoln explained, you must first reach his heart, the great high road to his reason.

—DORIS KEARNS GOODWIN

Trust is complex. *Britannica Online* defines trust as the ability to rely on a person's character, abilities, or truth-telling. A project management definition of trust is the confidence that a person or group can be depended upon to deliver on their commitments. Both are nice definitions, if a bit amorphous. It is more productive to think of trust as an interpersonal skill that can be developed, enhanced, or destroyed by careless actions.

Trust influences most aspects of large-scale project management and needs to be built into all your actions. Library projects often include people who don't work together for very long, and thus have difficulty developing trust in each other. In many instances, a project will have a communication person from one organization, technology people from one or more libraries, and a host of others from a consortium, the government, or elsewhere. For many national or international library projects, geography also influences how a group develops trust and increases the likelihood that cultural norms will not be in sync. Only rarely will any given team within a large project hierarchy have worked together in the past and built up trust over time.

As Anne DiPardo illustrates, the literature is filled with articles recommending that successful collaborations need time for team members to learn to trust each other enough so that when potential difficulties arise, they can be successfully resolved. A long-term study and review by J. Richard Hartman was designed to identify better ways of managing large-scale projects for the Canadian government. He looked at a range of project management tasks and found one common factor in the most successful ones. Trust was the key factor in better customer relations, time management, lower risks, and more effective communication.

Hartman identified three questions that underscore the foundations of trust:

1. Can this work be done on time and successfully?
2. Will my interests be heard and respected in this project?
3. Does this team relationship meet my needs?

These questions reveal how a project will impact the status of each participant. You need to help team members accurately gauge their status and role in the project. Being aware that the questions listed above are in the heads of the people around you can help you address these questions either overtly or in your actions and statements to the group.

You can demonstrate trust in your actions. The literature gives many examples of helpful behaviors:

- Listen respectfully, and repeat back what you heard to make sure you understood.

- Respect everyone's contributions, and do not allow ideas to be demeaned.
- Give authority to others, tell them exactly how they will be evaluated, and then hold them accountable.
- Talk straight when you can, be as transparent as possible, and acknowledge when you can't be open about a situation.
- Consider problems as learning opportunities, and ask what can be learned from this difficulty.
- Make sure team members have role and goal clarity; don't assume, but confirm this clarity.
- Be loyal, don't gossip, and acknowledge others' contributions and successes.
- Know the value of each person on the team and communicate those sentiments.
- Be accountable, accept and acknowledge your errors, and pledge to do better.
- Keep your commitments, and hold others to theirs.

And above all, achieve results, because this will go a long way to building trust.

Personality differences among librarians can often impact how groups function. I once attended a workshop of thirty-five librarians in which we took the DiSC Profiles testing system. In that group, 85 percent of attendees fell into either the "conscientious" or "dominant" personality profiles. This was surprising, since internationally those two types make up only 40 percent of the entire world's tested population. What became clear was that the workshop's set of librarians wanted to get things done with the least amount of touchy-feely actions or interpersonal interactions as possible. I bring this up because as a project manager you may be in a group of hard-driving achievers, as often happens in technology-focused projects, or you may be in a group of socially motivated librarians who are designing a new reference-based service model. While you aren't likely to be using profiling tools like DiSC Profiles (though this is not a bad idea), you should be aware that you need to meet the trust needs of a group of people with different motivations.

Having a trusting relationship with your project team allows you to function without the distraction of worrying too much about interpersonal conflicts, and a generally healthy emotional environment allows you to better navigate the problems that always come in a large-scale initiative. The reason you need trust is so you can rely on each other. Your collaborative project needs people who are comfortable sharing their ideas and knowledge. This is where psychological safety comes in.

LAUNCHING HEADFIRST INTO A SAFETY NET

Creating psychological safety is about giving candid feedback, openly admitting mistakes, and learning from one another.

—AMY EDMONDSON

Google spent two years studying nearly 200 teams to determine why some teams were more effective than others. They expected to find that a mix of the team members' traits and skills was the reason why some teams succeeded, and others didn't. Their hypothesis was wrong. It turned out that the traits and skills of team members didn't matter very much. What was important was how the team members interacted with each other, and how each person viewed his or her contribution to the group effort.

Google identified five related factors that impacted overall team performance:

- *Dependability*: you can trust that people will do what they say they will.
- *Structure/clarity*: both group goals and individual roles are clear, and meetings are well run.
- *Meaning*: the work is important to each team member at a personal level.
- *Impact*: the team members believe the work will make a difference.
- *Psychological safety*: the team is comfortable taking risks and admitting errors.

To everyone's surprise, Google found that feeling "psychological safety," or the willingness to take risks without fear of negative consequences, improved team performance more than any other factor.

Amy Edmondson has been one of the strongest supporters of the psychological safety concept, and I recommend her TED Talk on the topic. Psychological safety is found when team members feel safe with each other and are willing to risk vulnerability. According to Edmondson, no one wants to look ignorant, incompetent, intrusive, or overly negative. If team members feel unsafe, they withhold information and pay attention to how they appear rather than to what they are attempting to achieve. If a team has psychological safety, they do not fear being ridiculed, punished, or embarrassed for expressing their thoughts, concerns, and ideas. This allows dangerous or unwise decisions to be discovered early in a project.

Edmondson did significant research in hospital settings and found that the teams with the highest rating also had the highest number of reported errors. Why? Because those teams felt safe admitting to their mistakes, which allowed the errors to be corrected, and the team got better results with their next medical procedure.

To build psychological safety, Edmondson recommends framing your work as a learning problem. If you recognize that mistakes will happen and you can learn from them, mistakes can become a gift. You want to ask "how" and "what" questions. She recommends that team leaders acknowledge their errors and frequently ask, "Have we missed anything?" You can model curiosity by asking questions of team members, especially the quiet ones. Your goal should be to create an environment where people feel free to speak up.

People need to perceive that the groups they work in are fair, and if the playing field feels unfair, team members are likely to withdraw or start engaging in one-upmanship behaviors. We all want to work in an environment where we are respected, where our competence is judged fairly, and we have positive social status and some degree of autonomy. In the end, successful teams are all about trust.

TEAMS, TEAMS, TEAMS

Teamwork is the ability to work together toward a common vision . . . It is the fuel that allows common people to attain uncommon results.

—ANDREW CARNEGIE

According to the *Encyclopedia of Management,* most library project teams would be classified as "problem-solving teams." Problem-solving teams are formed when a problem arises, or a task needs to be completed. They typically are cross-functional, with members from different areas coming together to perform a task, solve a problem, or achieve an objective. In this age of pandemics, team meetings are more likely than not to be online. The advantage of online teams is the ability to gather talent across large geographic distances.

Collaborative technology tools like videoconferencing, online document-sharing, and project task-tracking software have become mainstays in project management. The task of building chemistry within an online, geographically dispersed group can be particularly challenging, and it can take significantly longer for teams to set their pace and form alignments. The *Encyclopedia of Management* cited research which found that the most critical factors for running a successful virtual team are trust, effective collaboration, and excellent communication.

In library settings, determining who will be on your team may not be your choice. If you're lucky, you can make recommendations. Often in large-scale projects, the politics of the participating organizations outweighs your specific needs. This dynamic can create a challenging situation, since you will need people with specific skill sets. You're also going to want highly motivated people who have a reputation for follow-through and high levels of emotional intelligence. In circumstances where you can't choose your team members, the best thing you can do is to create detailed job descriptions of the skills and traits you need and then work with the leaders of your participating organizations to find the best match. Most library leaders will be flexible if you make a strong needs-based case and they aren't facing an internal political situation.

Your teams will be made up of a variety of people with different skills, amounts of experience, types of training (including teamwork training), and interpersonal skills. If you only have a limited number of political cards to play to get the team you need, play those cards to get the best people possible on your leadership team or steering committee. Try to get librarians who will have your back and help you through the hard times ahead. Your other task forces are good places to put people you don't want on your project. That sounds harsh, but it's a common reality.

You may need to do some team training before starting the work, which will probably go over poorly with them. Most library staff dislike touchy-feely training like building better teams despite their relative success rates. Remember, the focus should stay on the project's mission and the goals! Library teams will veer off into processes and politics; your role is to bring them back to the goals and specific tasks. You may want to put a sign up in your office to remind you: *It's the mission, stupid!*

USING NORMS TO MANAGE TEAMS

Teamwork is neither "good" nor "desirable." It is a fact . . . Which team to use for what purpose is a crucial, difficult, and risky decision that is even harder to unmake.

—PETER DRUCKER

There are a handful of techniques that library project managers can use to improve the team process. The first is staying focused on the project's mission and goals. The second most important technique is to make sure your team has task clarity and knows what measures will be used to judge their success. You may want to let the team determine what measurements to use in their evaluation system.

You should keep meetings focused on the task at hand, not on process questions like the quality of the meeting minutes. If the meetings are to start at 1:00 p.m., then start at 1:00 p.m. sharp. People will complain, but they'll also appreciate the show of situational control. If reading a document is required for those attending the next meeting, tell them you will check in around the group before you start the discussion to make sure everyone has read it, and then do that. Unclear assignments or lack of follow-through are noted in project management literature for making a bad team environment.

Libraries have cultural norms, and so do projects. If your initiative crosses between public and academic libraries, you will have significant cultural differences to navigate, but cultural differences may also occur between rural and urban public libraries, or between universities and small community colleges. Your best bet is to develop your own group norms. What are the norms going to be for your project's working environment? Things like starting a meeting on time and requiring reading to be done before the meeting are examples of project norms.

You're going to need people with specific expertise and skills on your teams. There is a tricky balance here. You need to get the necessary expertise, but not let any given expert dominate. You will be balancing expert opinion, political expectations, and each library's needs throughout the process. My recommendation is that you acknowledge these situations with your teams, explain the conflicting elements, and settle for the best decision you can get under the circumstances.

Other successful team management techniques include:

- *Share success*: You can never give other people enough credit, and beware the one time you forget someone's contribution. The memory of missing credit lasts a long time.
- *Model curiosity*: Ask your team "how" and "why" questions, and listen intently to their responses. Bring the group's attention back to gracious listening if it wanders into sidebar conversations.
- *Size matters*: Richard Hackman found that smaller groups often do better than larger ones. He found that large teams allow the members to coast or loaf, and that can build resentment among those who are working hard. Smaller teams of five to seven members often are the most efficient.
- *Encourage personal involvement*: Amy Edmondson's work on psychological safety found that people need to have a personal interest in the project to be full contributors. Finding out the personal interests of your team members can help shape a healthy dynamic. At times, you can create a win-win situation when you match a team member's interests with one of the project's tasks. Ask questions like: What would you like to achieve on this project? What would be your best contribution? How can we optimize our work so that you (and your home organization) get the best results from your work on this team?

Richard Hackman has also looked closely at the myths we develop around working in teams. His number-one recommendation is that you shouldn't worry about how smoothly your colleagues interact. He found that well-managed conflict can generate more creativity and energy within a working group. Hackman isn't talking about toxic personal disagreements, but about reasoned disagreements about how the work is to be performed. If the team feels a passion to move the mission forward, it can sometimes be helpful to have a bumpy discussion.

There is a plethora of research on team management. Online courses from LinkedIn Learning and local universities, and videos, books, and journal articles abound on the subject. I recommend you look at work by Todd Dewett or Adrian Gostick on managing teams. Also, John Maxwell's well-known book *The 17 Indisputable Laws of Teamwork* has recently been revised. Patrick Lencioni has done some interesting work from a counter-intuitive perspective in *The Five Dysfunctions of a Team*. It may be worth your time to brush up on your team management skills with these sources.

FACILITATIVE LEADERSHIP

If you just put people together, they're going to crash and burn unless they have conflict resolution training, a manager who can coordinate roles, and opportunities to learn with one another.

—LINDY GREER

I considered starting this chapter with the concept of facilitative leadership because many project management books do that. I chose not to do this because I don't believe the role of the leader should be your number-one concern. This may sound contradictory given the sheer amount of work this book lays out for you to do, but the leader's role should never be the focus. The focus should always remain solidly locked on the project's mission and goals.

Think of leadership as using a series of tools that best meet the circumstances of your project. In one sense, facilitative leadership is another tool to achieve goal success. Furthermore, learning to be a collaborative leader is a process that takes time and practice. As you go through the many steps in large-scale project development, you will have plenty of opportunities to practice different leadership skills. I recommend you try many techniques to widen your leadership skills toolkit.

In facilitative leadership, the focus is on encouraging active involvement by the team members, having clear action plans, and demonstrating the ability to reach agreements. David Straus, the author of *How to Make Collaboration Work,* argues that one of the most important pieces of facilitative leadership is sharing an inspiring value. Librarianship is a value-based profession, and we respond to calls to our better nature. People work harder and with more commitment to projects that they believe in, and having a vision inspires them to make a difference.

Straus also argues that a facilitative project manager is juggling three balls at once:

1. *Results*: You are managing performance, timetables, resources acquisition, and a million other details that move your initiative forward.
2. *Processes*: You have a plan that you think will work, but as you move forward, you should constantly be scanning for ways to improve the process.

3. *Relationships*: Most facilitative leadership books focus on how you treat others. How inclusive are you, and how open to new ideas are you? How responsive are you to criticism? Can you respect everyone's point of view? Can you be humble and give away credit? You're going to want to end this project with more and deeper relationships than you started with.

There are various techniques associated with facilitative leadership. All of these techniques are valuable and worthy of being in your toolkit. I have found during several statewide projects that there were times when I needed to bring in a neutral facilitator to gather input or manage conflict between stakeholders. I needed to demonstrate that I was willing to minimize the impact of my biases, and using a neutral facilitator conveyed that message.

BURSTING THE BUBBLE

The world hates change, yet it is the only thing that has brought progress.

—CHARLES KETTERING

I have a working theory about success in libraries. I call it the 33-33-33 premise. I learned early in my career that you can't make everyone happy; if you try, you will be perceived as a flip-flopper. But I have always been someone who wanted to push the envelope. So how do you navigate so as to bring change to your organization? I've found the key is to have 33 percent of your colleagues or employees enthusiastic about the new project. Think of that group as your innovators or early adopters. Another 33 percent can hold back judgment or remain neutral; these are your early and late majority adopters. The final 33 percent will always be the laggards, who are opposed to any new idea. My best success has come when the laggard number was as low as 5–10 percent, but you can still make significant changes with a higher group of negative voices—it's just a lot harder to do.

It's easy when you are deep into implementing a large-scale initiative to get lost in the process, since you face a million moving parts and day-to-day problems. There is only so much time in a day, and sometimes it will feel like you're trapped in problem-solving and nothing gets done. You must keep your eyes on the entire project and what work you need to do to maintain both forward momentum and good working relationships. Look for others who can solve minor logistical problems or deal with committee disruptions. Keep your focus on the big picture and communicate, communicate, and then communicate again.

Think of how often modern American presidents are said to be in a bubble. Don't live in a bubble! Successful project managers build relationships with everyone involved in the process, whether on the job, in the break room, or at a social lunch. Don't get stuck listening to the same small pool of voices from your leadership team. You'll be spending most of your time with those people, so it will be your job to introduce input and insights from the wider community into that group's discussions.

REFERENCES

Atkinson, Jeremy. "Collaboration by Academic Libraries: What Are the Benefits, What Are the Constraints, and What Do You Need to Do to Be Successful?" *New Review of Academic Librarianship* 25 (2019): 1–7.

Delizonna, Laura. "High-Performing Teams Need Psychological Safety. Here's How to Create It." *Harvard Business Review Digital Articles* (August 24, 2017): 2–5.

Dewett, Todd. *Managing Teams.* Carpenteria, CA: LinkedIn Learning, 2013.

DiPardo, Anne. "Of War, Doom, and Laughter: Images of Collaboration in the Public-School Workplace." *Teacher Education Quarterly* 24 (1997): 89–104.

Edmondson, Amy. *The Fearless Organization: Creating Psychological Safety in the Workplace for Learning, Innovation, and Growth.* Hoboken, NJ: John Wiley & Sons, 2019.

———. "Psychological Safety and Learning Behavior in Work Teams." *Administrative Science Quarterly* 44 (1999): 350–83.

Encyclopedia of Management, 6th ed. Detroit, MI: Gale, 2009.

Gostick, Adrian, and Chester Elto. *The Best Team Wins: The New Science of High Performance.* New York: Simon & Schuster, 2018.

Hackman, J. Richard. *Leading Teams: Setting the Stage for Great Performances.* Boston: Harvard Business School Press, 2002.

Hartman, F. T. "The Role of Trust in Project Management." In *Frontiers of Project Management Research*, 225–35. Project Management Institute, 2002.

Lencioni, Patrick. *The Five Dysfunctions of a Team: A Leadership Fable.* San Francisco: Jossey-Bass, 2002.

Machovec, George. "What Library Collaboration Means to Me: Perspectives from an Academic Consortium Director." *Collaborative Librarianship* 11 (2019): 140–43.

Maxwell, John C. *The 17 Indisputable Laws of Teamwork: Embrace Them and Empower your Team.* Nashville, TN: Thomas Nelson, 2003.

Straus, David. *How to Make Collaboration Work: Powerful Ways to Build Consensus, Solve Problems, and Make Decisions.* San Francisco: Berrett-Koehler, 2002.

OWN YOUR LAUNCH!

GETTING READY TO RIDE

When you're getting ready to launch into space, you're sitting on a big explosion waiting to happen.

—SALLY RIDE

The best libraries know how to sell their services. This chapter looks at the power of proudly owning the audacity of your big idea and reminding everyone how it can transform lives and libraries going into the future. Only those who have launched large initiatives can know the terror that intensifies as you approach your go-live date. So many hours, so many plans, so many people, so much money have all been spent. If you're honest, you don't know if it's going to work. You may believe your project will succeed, but you never know until it's live. It's time to buckle up and ride.

ROLLING IT OUT, SOFTLY

[The pilot launch] separates goals from implementation and gives everybody a face-saving moment.

—ELLIS BOOKER

A "soft launch" is magic, whether it is named a pilot, a beta test, or a trial. Soft launches tell everyone that we're in test mode, that things can change. A soft launch allows you to test your hypothesis and determine the feasibility of implementing your full project at a later point. Soft launches are a way of managing risks and identifying deficiencies while protecting reputations and giving space for problems to be fixed. In my career, I have not seen any downside to using one of the soft launch techniques.

A soft rollout means you will release the new project with little or no fanfare. You may have a predetermined set of librarians and patrons ready to test out the new product's features. Generally, the version released in a soft rollout is a nearly completed version of the system. You gain the benefit of an evaluation without having to face public scrutiny. Given that user testing is a well-known phenomenon, if word gets out about problems, you'll have a cloak of protection, since you can continue to improve the product before the full launch.

If you don't have a big advertising budget, a slow rollout will also allow you to use time and carefully managed supporters' comments to build publicity about the new product. The classic example of this slow buildup was Google's GMAIL, which was released early in 2005 in beta test but was not officially "live" until late 2006. This delay allowed Google to continue to improve the product, while enticing early adopters to help evaluate the system so that they would become public advocates. If you have identified a group of supporters who are willing to spend time helping you develop and evaluate your product, you have identified a core of invested individuals who can be your spokespeople. You will recall that Everett Rogers found that the most powerful tool for marketing was word of mouth by members within a known community.

When choosing a soft launch method, the project manager factors in the cost of the project versus its perceived chances of success. You might select a different type of launch based on the nature of the project. For example, when considering launching a new database, most libraries use the trial methodology, since the ongoing costs of supporting an expensive database make it important that patrons understand that the product may not be available forever.

Trial

Trials explore whether the assumptions you made during the project implementation are viable, as well as helping manage risk by providing a buffer of time for more experimentation. Of all the categories, trials announce the clearest that this product is temporary, and access will end at a specific announced date. The product might come back but for now, it's temporary. As previously mentioned, trials are almost universally used in libraries when looking at high-ticket products like databases or learning support systems.

Given their temporary nature, when setting up a trial, it is important to announce the end date in public messaging. Trials typically seek a broad base of user input and are often heavily advertised to test to see if there is an audience for the product. Officially announced trials often include an online survey to solicit user feedback. On the negative side, the temporary nature of a trial—like that of a soft rollout—can strain staff, since the uncertainty about the future prohibits realigning workflows to provide the best customer service. Trials are effective risk management strategies but should be used with caution, since the assumption that the service or product will go away at some point can annoy some patrons who want access to it.

Pilot

A pilot project is an initial, often small-scale implementation of a new product or service that is typically shared with a limited user base. Pilots are used to prove system viability and have appeal to a specific population of patrons. There is an assumption when using a pilot that it can be canceled with no harm to the initiators. Pilots tend to be common in software rollouts when there is concern about how quickly the system can scale up to meet growing demand. Choose the term *pilot* when you are reasonably certain the project will succeed, but you might want to adjust its design features. A pilot gives you room to make changes with minimal irritation.

Pilots are often tied to what is called "proof of concept." According to Rick Anderson, proof of concept shows that a theory can survive real-life applications. As he says, "a pilot program demonstrates proof of concept by showing in the real world that, yes, one's library can develop, host, and maintain an open educational resource (OER); or establish a house-published journal and produce as least one issue; or provide a home for a digital archive; or establish an award for outstanding student service." Libraries, as publicly funded entities, are usually required to demonstrate feasibility, and a pilot is a strong, public-facing way to do that.

Beta Testing

A beta test is the final stage of the development of software or some other product. While the term *beta test* originated in software development circles, its common usage has extended to any rollout of a new, mostly untried system. In general, beta versions are opened to external users with the express purpose of searching for significant errors in a program, testing how easy the design features are to use, and allowing a small subset of users to have some say in the development path. The main difference between a pilot project and a beta test is the assumption that during a beta test, significant efforts will be made to gain feedback about the usability of the system. Think of a beta test as more of a two-way street where both the developers and users have responsibilities that must be met.

The use of any soft launch strategy can significantly reduce risks when launching a new, expensive, innovative, large-scale initiative. Such a strategy enables your project team to get a better handle on important usage and design features. These tests can serve as a first-level project evaluation system as well. Moreover, the knowledge learned can help clarify future messaging. But as strongly as I encourage using a soft launch strategy, there may be times when a dramatic public launch serves your needs better.

GO LIVE OR GO HOME

The success of the Go Live day is measured by the lack of problems.

—STEPHEN HARWOOD

The phrase *go-live date* is often used in project management literature for the day when the switch is flipped, and the new system is up and running for everyone. *Going live* means to make the launch happen; that is, to make the new product, service, or system fully available to the public. This will be the *big* milestone on your planning charts! You are saying your project is now available to the widest possible user population.

There are many activities that take place behind the scenes before a go-live event. I've created numerous go-live checklists, in which the details that must be handled before the system goes public are identified and checked off as they are completed. These often-lengthy checklists include the fundamentals from your project plan, but also details about the public relations and the celebratory party after you're up and running. There are numerous examples of go-live checklists online, but in my experience each project is unique, so it may be best to assign this activity to a go-live task force.

The Full Monty

We may not be young, we may not be pretty, we may not be right good, but we're here, we're live and for one night only, we're going for the Full Monty!

—FROM *THE FULL MONTY* MOVIE

There are times when you want to go for the gusto on your official "go-live" day, and you want a splashy public relations blitz. If you're confident your project is stable and doesn't need tweaking, and you've tested the service or product behind the scenes and are happy with the feedback, then going all-in on the launch can pay off. The primary payoff is that you will never have more attention or free publicity than when you first open your doors to the public. Going out there with a big launch proclaims to the world that you have a lot of confidence in your new system.

In April 2013, the Digital Public Library of America went for an all-out blitz to announce its historic digital collection to the world. The DPLA earned enormous free publicity from that decision, which drove usage on its system for years to come. The big launch fit its mission of being a "national resource" that was intended to reach as many libraries and users as possible. The DPLA launched with a sizable collection of over 2 million digital records from 500 institutions and quickly grew afterward. In Boston, they held the first DPLAFest event to draw attention to the launch. Unfortunately, the Boston Marathon tragedy forced some changes to their programming, but in the end, it spread out the festivities over a longer time frame, thus earning even more free publicity.

Marketing to libraries was a big part of the DPLA's launch, since they hoped that every library would add the DPLA collection to its website and thus expand the collection's reach. They developed a shareable elevator speech that told the world what the DPLA was. The DPLA cleverly used analogies to help explain the new service and how the collection matched the worldview of librarians. In press releases they said: "In much the same way that you might find a book not available at your local library through an interlibrary loan system, DPLA will link digital collections from across the United States to make a wide variety of content directly available to users."

Dan Cohen, the DPLA's first director, asked during numerous events: "Is there anything better than walking into a library for the first time, the wonder and joy of having so much knowledge and history and entertainment at one's fingertips?" The DPLA hosted a huge party on April 18 at the Boston Public Library with luminaries such as ALA President Maureen Sullivan. Spectacular historical photos were projected on the side of the library. Twitter ran crazy with positive comments, and the DPLA website experienced a half-million views per hour in the first days after the launch. Organizers claimed to have engaged with more than 1,000 people in libraries, publishing, technology businesses, government entities, and funding institution in preparation for their splashy launch.

If you're lucky, you'll never have to do a big launch during a national tragedy. But it turned out well for the DPLA, proving the old adage claims that "fortune favors the bold." If you feel your system is stable, appealing, and ready for heavy usage, then choosing the "full monty" launch approach may be your best bet.

LOGROLLING AND OTHER LAUNCH HAZARDS

After the launch phase, your product is old news. Take advantage of the opportunity to generate interest when your product is new.

—BRIAN LAWLEY

There are potential hazards in any rollout—soft, hard, or otherwise. There is a high probability that something will go wrong during a rollout. You have two choices: you can warn participants and interested parties that bad things might happen in advance and thus potentially arouse less enthusiasm; or you can wait until problems occur, and then hope to fix them fast enough that the reputational damage is held to a minimum. Before your go-live date is a good time to ask your stakeholders for a show of support. Take time to make sure there aren't any misunderstandings among your various stakeholders and key participants. Those weeks as you prepare for your go-live date are a good time to test out your marketing and messaging strategies in your participant community.

As part of the large team that worked on SimplyE (the New York Public Library's e-book reader app), I can attest that we went through numerous market concepts as we struggled to understand the difficulties of launching a library-created e-book app. Would it work for midsized libraries? Would it work for academics? Would it work for a cultural heritage organization? Looking back at the vast array of public programs and articles we produced in those first few years, our messaging was all over the place. It was exciting, but it was also messy. We suffered somewhat from the dazzle of the system's potentialities. Eventually, the reality that this system was going to work best for either large and medium-sized public libraries or for well-established consortia of public libraries became clear and our messaging stabilized and became more effective.

Finally, consider the advice of LinkedIn founder Reid Hoffman. He said: "If you're not embarrassed by your first product release, you've launched too late. Everyone wants their product to be shiny, great, and revolutionary, so they take too long in the development cycle to build this really shiny thing, when in fact time matters." Only you and your team know when to launch. What is required of you is to consider all the factors that go into timing a launch. Decide whether you're more comfortable launching early with bugs in the system, or launching too late and risking that no one cares anymore. Or you can try to find the sweet spot in the middle. Project management is all about trade-offs. The go-live date will be one of the more memorable trade-off decisions you make as project manager.

HYPE THE PROJECT

I think of the Gartner Hype Cycle as mostly a reflection of industry consensus.

—MICHAEL MULLANY

You've launched with a core group of supporting libraries. If you are lucky, this group is large enough to sustain your project long into the future. Unfortunately, that would be the exception, not the rule. Most large-scale library projects need to gain new participants to continue to be financially and politically viable. Now that your system is up and running smoothly, it's time to grow.

The Gartner Hype Cycle was named after the Gartner information technology firm, which developed the concept in 1995. It explains how new technologies move from launch to extensive participation. While it began in the technology field, the hype cycle has become widely used to describe marketing strategies for many new products and services. It should not be thought of as a path that all technology follows, but rather more of a consensus on what many technology adopters have experienced when launching new products. The model is not based on research, but more on perception and experience.

The hype cycle has five phases:

1. *Innovation Triggering* (formerly called technology trigger): This occurs at a breakthrough moment—a public demonstration, a launch, or some other event that calls attention to your initiative. Before this point, it was probably only a small group of in-the-loop innovators and early adopters who were paying attention. With the triggering event, there is often a swift uptake in media and social media interest. Once the buzz is on, more people will demand information.

2. *Peak of Inflated Expectations*: All that early attention creates the assumption of success despite the actual capacities of your new system. A bandwagon effect can take place, with people wanting to join in who may or may not be good candidates for participation.

3. *Trough of Disillusionment*: Even with a perfect product launch, interest over time will wane, especially if the new system hasn't delivered on inflated expectations. Most new services have initial problems with performance, improve slower than anticipated, or worst of all, aren't seen as delivering meaningful value. This is a time when your active participants and stakeholders must openly support the project in order to help maintain its forward momentum.

4. *Slope of Enlightenment*: Your technology is starting to work, and its true value is better understood. This stage can include participants having found unexpected uses for the new product. Updates and improvements are planned and announced, funding has stabilized, and more late majority adopters are joining in.

5. *Plateau of Productivity*: Adoption of the product is approaching mainstream acceptance. Assessments of the new product are generally positive, and its functionality is clearly understood. The payoff is occurring for participants.

The value of the Gartner Hype Cycle is that it lets you foresee the insanities that occur as large-scale initiatives move from development into real-world applications. The hype cycle has been criticized for its use of colorful language like "disillusionment" and "enlightenment," but those terms are also seen as a strength by many because they provide clarity to the often-ridiculous expectations that can build up following a new product launch.

You should gather from the hype cycle that your audience, in their enthusiasm, may possess expectations that become inflated or unrealistic. At some point, after those expectations have been deflated, the audience may even move into some level of unhappiness with your project. The good news is that many projects find a way back up from this low point to demonstrate their value to stakeholders. The hype cycle is also meant to remind us that the target audiences for our project may change from the originally intended vision. As the product is found to be useful in other, unintended ways, new users may appear.

COMMUNITY REPRESENTATIVES

The responsibilities of our Community Representatives help ensure the success of the program. Change-the-world isn't officially in the job description, but it does come with the territory.

—AYUSA.COM

Another effective technique for getting the word out about your project is to use "community representatives" or "ambassadors." Everett Rogers's "diffusion of innovation" research found that word of mouth from influential people within an in-group was the most effective way to generate interest and gain attention. Using a community representative is an effective tool for managing word-of-mouth publicity.

The DPLA in its earliest days chose to create a volunteer pool of community reps (their abbreviation). Their stated goal was to help raise public awareness of the DPLA across the country. The community reps were drawn from state libraries, public and academic libraries, K–12 schools, publishing houses, museums, the mass media, and genealogy organizations. In 2018 the DPLA had more than 100 active, volunteer ambassadors in nearly 40 states, and an additional 200 alumni. The charge given to the community reps was to:

1. Organize activities that promote the DPLA.
2. Share materials and feedback from DPLA outreach efforts such as blogs, videos, and publicity materials.
3. Confer with DPLA staff regarding their progress and share materials with other community reps.

The ambassadors also served as a sounding board to test educational materials, program agendas, usability studies, and promotional materials. The community reps were an active part of DPLA workshops and conferences and spoke frequently about the DPLA at regional conferences across the country.

The drawback to using community representatives is the amount of time required to maintain healthy relationships with these people across large geographic regions. A vetting process to make it prestigious to get a spot on the team of reps can help build buy-in, but active work must be undertaken to keep this enthusiastic pool of volunteers engaged. Moreover, you should not use the ambassador approach if you can't maintain your level of support for the program. Nothing is worse than bad marketing coming from disillusioned former fans. The White House Office of Consumer Affairs has stated that each dissatisfied customer tells as many as fifteen people about their negative experience.

REPORTING OUT

No one really wants to read a document. They just want to know what it says.

—ANONYMOUS BLOG POST

At the end of your big-splash launch, you will need to do a major report out to the participant community. A few months after the launch, when you've resolved most of your new product's significant problems, is the time to do a major project report. You'll be getting requests from stakeholders at this point for a full readout of the project. Typically, this report would include additional resources needed to keep the system going, any crises resolved and lessons learned, a clearer statement of the benefits of the initiative based on the early assessment of user responses, a statement of the system's long-term viability, a path for further refinement, and the plan for the next, more comprehensive level of evaluation. This report shows that you are up-front in your project assessment and you've attained the system maturity to make strong statements about the future.

THE PARTY'S OVER

As a project manager, there's a way to develop enthusiasm so meaningful and profound that it will not decline no matter what strain it is put under.

—ALFONSO BUCERO

After any launch, successful or not, there is a natural waning of enthusiasm in most large-scale projects. This inertia can put the project manager in a tough place, since the assumption will be that it is their job to keep everyone engaged and enthusiastic. If you have ever tried to make a tired two-year-old happy, you'll have a good handle on how hard it is to maintain excitement as things move toward normalization and are handed off to a maintenance group.

There are two strategies for dealing with waning enthusiasm. One is to just keep doing what you are doing. Sheer doggedness can get you through the last mile when everyone is tired, and the fun part is over. My other suggestion is to remember that projects are learning opportunities. Take some time to work with your teams on what they've learned, how they've changed or grown, and what they will avoid in the future. This resettling into a learning stance can add positive value to the project without the need to generate more hype.

REFERENCES

Anderson, Rick. "Proof of Concept, Proof of Program, and Proof of Scale in Scholarly Communication." *The Scholarly Kitchen* (blog), September 22, 2015.

Fenn, Jackie, and Mark Raskino. *Mastering the Hype Cycle: How to Choose the Right Innovation at the Right Time.* Boston: Harvard Business Press, 2008.

Hoffman, Reid, and Chris Yeh. *Blitzscale: The Lightning-Fast Path to Building Massively Valuable Companies.* New York: Currency, 2018.

Palfrey, John. "What Is the DPLA?" *Library Journal* 138 (2013): 38.

Thomas, Andrew. The Secret Ratio That Proves Why Customer Reviews Are So Important: It's what you don't know that hurts you. *Inc.com* (February 26, 2018).

Weinraub, Lajoie, Evviva Bridges, and Laurie Bridges. "Innovation Decisions: Using the Gartner Hype Cycle." *Library Leadership & Management* 28 (September 2014): 1–7.

ELEVEN

CLOSING THE LOOP

THE BEGINNING OF THE END

A glance at the development of the library idea will enable us better to predict its future, as the astronomer computes an orbit, not be study of where a body stands today, but of the track over which it has just come.

—MELVIL DEWEY

The journey you have been on from ideation to project launch has been an amazing one, and to be honest, sometimes a lonely one. While you've worked with hundreds of people, the burden for shepherding the project through to completion has been yours. There are many librarians who have done project management, but the pool of those who have led large-scale initiative work is quite small. Congratulations! You have joined a small, elite group of librarians. You'll find that your peers at this level are among the best and brightest the profession has to offer.

The project management stages you have completed are initiation, planning, and executing. The last two stages—monitoring/assessment and closing—remain to be done. I've found these to be the most difficult stages of the project management process, even though they are less labor-intensive ones. There was so much energy and enthusiasm in the initiation and planning stages, which was followed by the hard work of the executing stage, and which culminated in the big launch. Now the system is up and running, minor problems are being resolved, and new participants are trickling in. It's all good, but it doesn't have the same excitement as the earlier stages.

As a project manager, you must dig deep to find the energy reserves to keep the project process on track. There are still tasks to be done before you hand off the project to the group that will maintain the system over the long term. Each large-scale initiative will have a unique handover process. Some projects will go to an individual library to maintain, others to a library consortium or other partner organization, and some may branch out into a new nonprofit organization. Throughout the development of the project, discussions have been going on at the governance and leadership levels about what happens after the active phases of the project have ended. Project managers typically don't have a big say in who takes over the system, since this decision tends to be a political one.

The Project Management Institute recommends an article by Sheilina Somani on managing the emotional impact that closing a project has on both yourself and your teams. According to Somani, when initiatives close, the participants feel a range of emotions from grief, sadness, and loss to relief, delight, and euphoria. Following the final two steps of the project management process—assessment and closure—you and your participants need to let go of the project and move on.

One last time-consuming task remains, however: that of evaluating everything. Now is the time to evaluate how the project process went. More importantly, it is time to test your belief in the value of the project. Did it do what it intended? What are the lessons left to learn? The sheer size of the large-scale initiative can mask many positive benefits that accrued at the individual level. Be prepared, because the assessment stage will reveal many surprising details.

THE THREE-PROOF PROBLEM

All of these programs, products, or initiatives, if they want to become going concerns, have one challenge in common: all must demonstrate initial feasibility and ongoing sustainability.

—RICK ANDERSON

Rick Anderson in a *The Scholarly Kitchen* blog post identified three measures for evaluating large-scale library initiatives. He was talking about scholarly publishing, but the three measures can apply to any library system. Anderson's three proofs are proof of concept, proof of program, and proof of scale.

Proof of Concept

Did your big idea work? Did it successfully launch in the real world? Did librarians and patrons find value in it? Anderson claims that the pilot program is the most often-used vehicle for showing proof of concept. Initially, you are not necessarily looking for an avalanche of new users, but you need to see an increase in use over time.

When we launched the Minnesota Libraries Publishing Project, there was a lot of skepticism about whether there was a market for a statewide self-publishing platform supported by the state's libraries. There were real questions about the viability of our big idea, but these were disproved by our success. I remember one brilliant academic dean admitting to being shocked after learning that 20–30 new self-published books were being opened on the platform each month. Sometimes the only way to prove a concept is to do the concept.

Earlier in the book we discussed Guy Kawasaki's argument that innovation is a leap of belief. He rejects the old adage, "I'll believe it when I see it." Instead, he argues that "if you believe it, you can see it. That's how innovation happens. You need to buy in and believe that it works first." Kawasaki argues that no users of your system will ever tell you to create a revolution. They're only going to want you to make today's product better, faster, and cheaper. Sometimes you must take a big, creative leap to reach the next level.

Proof of Program

Rick Anderson's second evaluative criterion is proof of program. Here you are demonstrating that your project is sustainable. Could the Minnesota Libraries Publishing Project keep adding twenty self-published books a month to its platform? The answer turned out to be yes, it could. However, since no one else had ever launched a statewide book self-publishing platform, we had no way of knowing if the program was sustainable until we had gotten it up and running.

A question to keep in mind here is: You may be able to demonstrate proof of program because you continue to advertise and push the program to the public. But will your project remain sustainable if it is merely maintained, and no longer advertised? You need to know how much effort is required to keep it going. Another proof of concept question is, will others pick up your idea and replicate it? I knew the Minnesota Libraries Publishing Project would thrive when the Washington state librarian cited it as an example of the future of libraries to a packed auditorium at an ALA Annual Conference. You should consider writing about your project in library literature, as well as hitting the conference stage, in order to spread the word into the wider library community.

Proof of Scale

Anderson's final evaluative criterion is proof of scale. Will the use of the new system continue to grow, helping to create a sustainable financial model? Look no further than the Digital Preservation Network to see a cooperative library program that launched well, grew for quite a few years, and then saw a rapid decline in membership, forcing its closure. In a thoughtful article on the long-term sustainability of library collaboratives, Roger Schonfeld said in *The Scholarly Kitchen*: "It seems clear that we are in a period of instability for collaborative library community efforts, and more major changes are surely on the horizon."

Schonfeld and Anderson's arguments illustrate the unfortunate fact that sometimes the only way to survive is to take risks and push for growth. The goal is to have a large enough resource pool that if things go wrong, your system will not be in jeopardy. The reality of any cooperative library initiative is that participants will leave, but hopefully, new ones will also come in. To demonstrate proof of scale, you need to demonstrate the ability to grow and thus maintain financial viability.

Anderson's three proofs demonstrate that a project needs an audience, stable participants, and a path to future growth. The reality behind any library project is that you need to demonstrate growth over time, and nothing helps growth as much as growth. This is not a joke; for each project, there is a point when the number of participants tells the wider world: Hey! This project is viable, let's look at it. That number will vary depending on the project. For instance, a shared online catalog will need a smaller number of participants than a nationwide digital library. We are a follow-the-leader profession, so find your innovators and early adopters and march on.

PRODUCTIVITY MEASURES

If you can't measure it, you can't improve it.

—PETER DRUCKER

The *Online Dictionary for Library and Information Science (ODLIS)* defines an "output measure" as a quantifiable standard for assessing the work accomplished in order to help evaluate the effectiveness of a given library program or project. An example of an output measure is the number of books circulated in a given time period. An input measure, according to *ODLIS*, is a quantitative measure for judging the "extent of resources provided in support" of a library project, primarily for cost-analysis purposes. An example would be the average cost of purchasing, cataloging, and preparing a book for circulation. Libraries are overflowing with input and output measures.

The *Encyclopedia of Management* defines "productivity" as the measure of outputs divided by inputs over time. Productivity measures help libraries determine how well their resources are being utilized, compared to other libraries. Library managers find great value in looking at these measures across organizations in order to judge the individual performance of any given library service. These measures are often shared with funders to demonstrate the wise use of public funds.

Productivity measures will be necessary and expected from your project. However, it can be difficult to find any institution with which to compare your work when doing an innovative, large-scale library initiative. We ran into this dilemma with the Minnesota Libraries Publishing Project. As I said, we were seeing 20–30 new self-published books launched each month. Is that a good number? Who knows? No one else was doing that kind of work, and comparing a self-publishing project to a commercial publishing entity seemed inappropriate. We decided to think it was a great number and publicized it widely. Sometimes how you present your measures is more important than the actual numbers themselves.

OUTCOME MEASURES

Measuring outcomes means new ways for libraries to demonstrate their effectiveness.

—PROJECTOUTCOME.ORG

An *outcome* measures the benefits to individuals and communities from library activities. The ALA's Project Outcome claims that libraries collect massive amounts of data about their programs and services, but that data seldom illustrates a direct benefit to individuals or the community. In response, librarians have been working toward adopting more outcome-oriented measures. An example of an outcome measure is evaluating the value of a library's community literacy program based on it's impact on the local unemployment rate.

Outcome measures can be qualitative or quantitative and are often difficult to obtain. The reason why libraries struggle to measure outcomes is that it's harder to quantify a change in someone's life circumstances than it is to record the number of books that circulate. Project Outcome established four criteria: knowledge, confidence, application, and awareness to gauge the impact. As the Project Outcome website says, "measuring outcomes helps libraries answer the question, 'What good did we do?'"

The tools that are used to assess learning outcomes include pre- and post-testing, surveys, interviews, and the evaluation of research activities and classwork like papers, portfolios, or class projects. To illustrate this point from an academic perspective, Indiana University's "Principles of Good Assessment" web page lists some features of the best outcome assessments:

- They separate different skills in order to determine which ones are strong and which need more intervention.
- They test in ways that reveal the students' thinking, and how they come up with their answers.
- They have rubrics which show what excellent, good, average, and poor responses look like.
- They can be reused within a course.
- They may be graded.

You can see from this list how much effort must go into measuring student success outcomes. Outcomes seldom are a quick count, but outcome assessments are powerful tools that can demonstrate a library's or a project's effectiveness to the funder, governing entities, stakeholders, and the wider community. From the beginning when you established your project plan, you should have defined what outcomes you will measure. As you go along, you should set up procedures that will allow you to measure your results.

There are many excellent sources for deciding how your project should be assessed. In library literature, consider looking at Joseph R. Matthews's *The Evaluation and Measurement of Library Services*, Leo Appleton's *Libraries and Key Performance Indicators: A Framework for Practitioners*, and an older but still viable title, Hernon and Dugan's *Outcomes Assessment in Your Library*. Also, check out the ALA's academic and public library divisions' web pages for excellent referrals to the best measurement resources, as well as resources from the ALA's Project Outcome and the Measures that Matter websites.

EVALUATING THE PROJECT

Project evaluation appraises the progress and performance of the job compared to what was originally intended.

—JAMES P. LEWIS

The previous sections looked at assessing how your project impacted users of the new system. You also need to assess the project process itself. Here is where you evaluate the quality of the project management activities undertaken and how well the project's collaborative aspects worked.

In evaluating a project's process and performance, you are asking questions like the following:

- Did the project meet the assigned scope statement, including its specific functionality?
- How well did the project's execution match the assumptions in the project plan?
- What role did the leaders play in implementing the project throughout? (These "leaders" could also include governing entities, stakeholders, and participing libraries, if desired.)
- Did the project come in on time or at the agreed-upon adjusted deadline?
- Was the project completed within the budget or within an agreed-upon adjusted budget?
- What external, unforeseen factors impacted the project?
- How did the project leadership deal with problems and challenges?
- Were communications and outreach effective?
- Did the project launch effectively?

- Were the materials for staff training and public relations effective?
- Was the project process well documented?

This list is not meant to be comprehensive, but it gives you a starting point to design your own evaluation matrix.

A study by Jenn Anne Horwath did not find much evidence that libraries are doing a particularly good job of evaluating their projects. This deficiency is probably caused by insufficient knowledge of how to evaluate something as complex and fast-moving as a large project, coupled with the participants' fear that if problems are discovered, they will be judged harshly. All projects have problems and setbacks, however. Your evaluation should focus on how you overcame those problems rather than on the number of problems, with the caveat that problems caused by mismanagement are fair game.

Within project management literature, Willis Thomas's book *The Basics of Project Evaluation and Lessons Learned* is recommended. Having an external entity do the evaluation tends to add credibility to the results. Finally, the best evaluation systems are tied to systems that promote learning among project team members.

EVALUATING COLLABORATION

In an age of scarce resources, competition, and complex community issues—organizational collaboration is essential. However, the degree or level of collaboration necessary to counter and address these issues will vary and is dependent on the resources and vision of those that choose to work together.

—REBECCA GAJDA

Nowadays large-scale library projects tend to be collaborative, since partnerships are the only cost-effective method of achieving the goals. Given the critical nature of collaboration in library project management, it requires its own assessment considerations. Rebecca Gajda recommends using "collaboration theory" because it can help clarify what is meant by collaboration while giving a structure to the evaluation process. Evaluating collaborative efforts involves reaching out in dialogue with a wide range of participants and stakeholders.

There are questions unique to the collaborative aspect of a project that should be asked:

1. Did the partnerships advance the project's work plans?
2. Did we have the right partners? The right number of partners?
3. Did collaboration increase or decrease over the project's life cycle?
4. Did work processes among the partners become more integrated or remain autonomous?
5. Was the amount of time spent on the collaboration worth the time and resources expended?
6. Did learning occur among the partners?
7. Were there unexpected usages of the system discovered over time once it was launched?

Collaboration can be thought of as existing on a continuum from low interaction, communication, participation, and integration to high levels of the same. Given the assumption that it is desirable to have high levels of interaction, communication, participation, and integration, you can then ask how well the project achieved those results. You can develop a rubric where you look at levels of the criteria that best fit your collaborative needs, such as communication, interactions, and so on. Through dialogues, surveys, focus groups, and the like, you can determine whether you had a successful degree of collaboration on the project.

TURN IT OVER

I am not the only project manager who has failed to document their project.

—NAME WITHHELD

The final stage of the project management process is the closure stage. This is the stage where you turn your project over to maintenance personnel. This is also the stage that is easy to ignore and downplay. Typically, after the assessment stage is over, enthusiasm has continued to wane and you are phasing out employees, which can be discouraging. If you read a couple of project management books, you'll find a lot of sheepish authors talking about how they neglected this stage. My go-to expert, James P. Lewis, barely mentioned the closing process in his excellent book *Fundamentals of Project Management*.

If you're like most project managers, you've done a slipshod job of documentation, and now there is a compelling reason to get your documents in order. File-sharing software can help because all your minutes, plans, and other documents should be in one place online. The odds, however, are that while they're available they are *not* in an order that will make sense for those who come after you. Countless hours have been spent by project successors going over voluminous working files trying to find out when and why a decision was made and exactly what was agreed to. I've been there and done that!

After documentation, the other stages of the closeout process are:

1. Your final report summarizing everything learned from the evaluation of the system. The report should include an executive summary, the final status of the system, lessons learned, an overview of how the handover and maintenance process will work technically, and recommendations for improvement.
2. A final meeting with the governing entity, principal stakeholders, and other key personnel to highlight all remaining issues and make sure there is clarity about the status of the project handover.
3. Talking to team members about lessons learned from the feedback on the new system. This feedback can highlight important issues that will help with further maintenance of the system and will help the participants on their next project assignment.
4. Making sure that any vendor connections are passed on to the maintenance staff and vice versa.
5. Doing a press release at the point of handover. This is a time to highlight the success of the project and clarify any new communication channels that will be needed by ongoing participants.
6. Officially handing over ownership of the project to the new maintenance structure.

Finally, you should celebrate a job well done! Don't forget to recognize individual team members' contributions and let their supervisors know about the quality of their work.

THE END

You need a great idea, and you need great timing. But you also need hard work.

—BILL GATES

The handoff of a large, long-term library initiative to a maintenance group is going to be a bittersweet experience. If you are moving on to your next adventure, you have the added stress of saying goodbye to your colleagues and the friends you've made. The satisfying feelings of a job well done can only take you so far.

You may be remaining with the project as it goes into maintenance. Honestly, I hope you're not. Staying with the project will never feel the same as it did when you were creating it. But whether staying or going, the move into maintenance is a little sad and a little glorious. You've updated your resume and thanked what feels like a million people. My final recommendation to you is to take a moment and record what you learned. You can do what I did and write a book about it, or publish journal articles or give conference programs. Those acts will help you close out your amazing experience.

I will close this book out with a final quote from J. R. R. Tolkien's *The Hobbit*. "Go back?" he thought. "No good at all! Go sideways? Impossible! Go forward? Only thing to do! On we go!"

REFERENCES

Anderson, Rick. "Proof of Concept, Proof of Program, and Proof of Scale in Scholarly Communication." *The Scholarly Kitchen* (blog), September 22, 2015.

Appleton, Leo. *Libraries and Key Performance Indicators: A Framework for Practitioners*. Cambridge, MA: Chandos, 2017.

Gajda, Rebecca. "Utilizing Collaboration Theory to Evaluate Strategic Alliances." *American Journal of Evaluation* 25 (2016): 65–77.

Hernon, Peter, and Robert E. Dugan. *Outcomes Assessment in Your Library*. Chicago: American Library Association, 2002.

Horwath, Jenn Anne. "How Do We Manage? Project Management in Libraries: An Investigation." *Partnership: The Canadian Journal of Library and Information Practice and Research* 7 (2012): 1–34.

Kawasaki, Guy Takeo. *The Top 10 Mistakes of Entrepreneurs*. YouTube video, March 11, 2013.

Matthews, Joseph R. *The Evaluation and Measurement of Library Services*. Santa Barbara, CA: Libraries Unlimited, 2018.

Reitz, Joan M., ed. *Online Dictionary for Library and Information Science: ODLIS*. Westport, CT: Libraries Unlimited, 2005.

Schonfeld, Roger C. "Why Is the Digital Preservation Network Disbanding?" *The Scholarly Kitchen* (blog), December 13, 2018.

Somani, Sheilina. "Beginning of the End." *PM Network* 28 (2014): 25.

Thomas, Willis H. *The Basics of Project Evaluation and Lessons Learned*. 2nd ed. Boca Raton, FL: CRC Press, Taylor & Francis Group, 2015.

INDEX